Table of contents

Ethical codes and declarations relevant to the health professions

Introduction

This compilation brings together international ethical codes and declarations relevant to the work of health professionals in the field of human rights. They come from a number of sources:

- from Amnesty International itself (Declaration on the Participation of Health Personnel in the Death Penalty; Declaration of Stockholm; and the three programs for the prevention of torture, extrajudicial executions and disappearances);

- from the United Nations (Principles of Medical Ethics; Convention against Torture; Principles on the Effective Prevention and Investigation of Extra-legal, Arbitrary and Summary Executions; Principles for the Protection of Persons with Mental Illness; Body of Principles for the Protection of All Persons under Any Form of Detention or Imprisonment; Standard Minimum Rules);

- from the World Medical Association (Declaration of Geneva; Resolution on Physician Participation in the Death Penalty; International Code of Medical Ethics; Regulations in Time of Armed Conflict; Declaration of Tokyo; Declaration of Malta on Hunger Strikers);

- from the World Psychiatric Association (Declaration of Hawaii; Declaration on the Participation of Psychiatrists in the Death Penalty);

- from the International Council of Nurses (Role of the Nurse in the Care of Prisoners and Detainees; the Nurse's Role in Safeguarding Human Rights; Statement on the Death Penalty and Participation by Nurses in Executions; Statement on Nurses and Torture);

- from the Geneva Conventions;

- from the International Council of Prison Medical Services (Oath of Athens);

- from the International Union of Psychological Science (ethical statement);

1

• and from antiquity (The Hippocratic Oath).

Amnesty International is reproducing them in this collection for use and reference by health professionals working on human right concerns. Although the declarations and principles are not enforceable in a court of law, they nevertheless represent an international consensus and carry unquestionable moral authority. They should be used whenever it is appropriate to refer to the medical ethical dimension of human rights. (The Convention Against Torture and the Geneva Conventions differ since they are *binding* on states party to the conventions.)

Health professionals have been active in the work of Amnesty International since its inception in 1961 and have played an increasingly valuable role in documenting human rights abuses, arranging treatment for victims of such abuses, and campaigning for the observance, and indeed the strengthening, of human rights and ethical standards. This compilation is intended to contribute to the effectiveness of such work.

Statements by professional associations

Physicians

- Declaration of Geneva

- Resolution on physician participation in capital punishment

- International code of medical ethics

- Regulations in time of armed conflict

- Declaration of Tokyo

- Declaration of Malta on hunger strikers

The Declaration of Geneva
(World Medical Association, 1948, 1968, 1983)

The World Medical Association was formed in 1947. High on its list of priorities was the formulation of the modern equivalent of the Hippocratic Oath. First adopted by the Second World Medical Assembly in 1948, the Declaration of Geneva was amended by the 22nd Assembly of the WMA meeting in Sydney, Australia in 1968, by the 35th World Medical Assembly meeting in Venice, Italy in 1983 and, again, by the 46th Assembly in Stockholm in 1994. The text, as amended, reads as follows:

Declaration of Geneva

At the time of being admitted as a member of the medical profession:

I solemnly pledge myself to consecrate my life to the service of humanity;

I will give to my teachers the respect and gratitude which is their due;

I will practice my profession with conscience and dignity;

The health of my patient will be my first consideration;

I will respect the secrets which are confided in me, even after the patient has died;

I will maintain by all the means in my power, the honor and the noble traditions of the medical profession;

My colleagues will be my sisters and brothers;

I will not permit considerations of age, disease or disability, creed, ethnic origin, gender, nationality, political affiliation, race, sexual orientation or social standing to intervene between my duty and my patient;

I will maintain the utmost respect for human life from its beginning even under threat and I will not use my medical knowledge contrary to the laws of humanity;

I make these promises solemnly, freely and upon my honour.

International Code of Medical Ethics
(World Medical Association, 1949, 1968, 1983)

Drawing on the Declaration of Geneva, the WMA formulated a more detailed code of ethics which was approved by the 3rd Assembly of the WMA meeting in London in 1949. The International Code of Medical Ethics was subsequently amended in 1968 by the 22nd Assembly of the WMA in Sydney and again in 1983 by the 35th Assembly held in Venice. The text, as amended, reads as follows:

International Code of Medical Ethics

Duties of Physicians in General

A physician shall always maintain the highest standards of professional conduct.

A physician shall not permit motives of profit to influence the free and independent exercise of professional judgement on behalf of patients.

A physician shall, in all types of medical practice, be dedicated to providing competent medical services in full technical and moral independence, with compassion and respect for human dignity.

A physician shall deal honestly with patients and colleagues, and strive to expose those physicians deficient in character or competence, or who engage in fraud or deception.

The following practices are deemed to be unethical conduct:

a) Self advertising by physicians, unless permitted by the laws of the country and the Code of Ethics of the National Medical Association.
b) Paying or receiving any fee or any other consideration solely to procure the referral of a patient or for prescribing or referring a patient to any source.

A physician shall respect the rights of patients, of colleagues, and of other health professionals, and shall safeguard patient confidences.

A physician shall act only in the patient's interest when providing medical care which might have the effect of weakening the physical and medical condition of the patient.

A physician shall use great caution in divulging discoveries or new techniques or treatment through non-professional channels.

A physician shall certify only that which he has personally verified.

Duties of Physicians to the Sick

A physician shall always bear in mind the obligation of preserving human life.

A physician shall owe his patients complete loyalty and all the resources of his science. Whenever an examination or treatment is beyond the physician's capacity he should summon another physician who has the necessary ability.

A physician shall preserve absolute confidentiality on all he knows about his patient even after the patient has died.

A physician shall give emergency care as a humanitarian duty unless he is assured that others are willing and able to give such care.

Duties of Physicians to each other

A physician shall behave towards his colleagues as he would have them behave towards him.

A physician shall not entice patients from his colleagues.

A physician shall observe the principles of the "Declaration of Geneva" approved by the World Medical Association.

Regulations in Time of Armed Conflict
(World Medical Association, 1956, 1957, 1983)

These regulations or guidelines set out the WMA's standards on the medical ethical position of the physician during a period of war or other armed conflict. The statement was approved by the 10th World Medical Assembly in Havana in 1956, was edited by the 11th Assembly meeting in Istanbul the following year and amended by the 35th World Medical Assembly in 1983. The amended text reads as follows:

Regulations in Time of Armed Conflict

1. Medical ethics in time of armed conflict is identical to medical ethics in time of peace, as established in the International Code of Medical Ethics of the World Medical Association. The primary obligation of the physician is his professional duty; in performing his professional duty, the physician's supreme guide is his conscience.

2. The primary task of the medical profession is to preserve health and save life. Hence it is deemed unethical for physicians to:

   A. Give advice or perform prophylactic, diagnostic or therapeutic procedures that are not justifiable in the patient's interest.

   B. Weaken the physical or mental strength of a human being without therapeutic justification.

   C. Employ scientific knowledge to imperil health or destroy life.

3. Human experimentation in time of armed conflict is governed by the same code as in time of peace; it is strictly forbidden on all persons deprived of their liberty, especially civilian and military prisoners and the population of occupied countries.

4. In emergencies, the physician must always give the required care impartially and without consideration of sex, race, nationality, religion, political affiliation or any other similar criterion. Such medical assistance must be continued for as long as necessary and practicable.

5. Medical confidentiality must be preserved by the physician in the practice of his profession.

7

6. Privileges and facilities afforded the physician must never be used for other than professional purposes.

Rules governing the care of sick and wounded, particularly in time of conflict

A. 1. Under all circumstances, every person, military or civilian, must receive promptly the care he needs without consideration of sex, race, nationality, religion, political affiliation or any other similar criterion.

   2. Any procedure detrimental to the health, physical or mental integrity of a human being is forbidden unless therapeutically justifiable.

B. 1. In emergencies, physicians and associated medical personnel are required to render immediate service to the best of their ability. No distinction shall be made between patients except those justified by medical urgency.

   2. The members of medical and auxiliary professions must be granted the protection needed to carry out their professional activities freely. The assistance necessary should be given to them in fulfilling their responsibilities. Free passage should be granted whenever their assistance is required. They should be afforded complete professional independence.

   3. The fulfilment of medical duties and responsibilities shall in no circumstance be considered an offence. The physician must never be prosecuted for observing professional secrecy.

   4. In fulfilling their professional duties, the medical and auxiliary professions will be identified by the distinctive emblem of a red serpent and staff on a white field. The use of this emblem is governed by special regulation.

The Declaration of Tokyo
(World Medical Association, 1975)

The Declaration of Tokyo has been, since its adoption in 1975, the most comprehensive statement produced by the medical profession on the question of torture and cruel, inhuman or degrading treatment of detainees. It was adopted by the 29th World Medical Assembly, Tokyo, Japan. The text is as follows.

Declaration of Tokyo

Preamble

It is the privilege of the medical doctor to practise medicine in the service of humanity, to preserve and restore bodily and mental health without distinction as to persons, to comfort and to ease the suffering of his or her patients. The utmost respect for human life is to be maintained even under threat, and no use made of any medical knowledge contrary to the laws of humanity.

For the purpose of this Declaration, torture is defined as the deliberate, systematic or wanton infliction of physical or mental suffering by one or more persons acting alone or on the orders of any authority, to force another person to yield information, to make a confession, or for any other reason.

1. The doctor shall not countenance, condone or participate in the practice of torture or other forms of cruel, inhuman or degrading procedures, whatever the offence of which the victim of such procedures is suspected, accused or guilty, and whatever the victim's beliefs or motives, and in all situations, including armed conflict and civil strife.

2. The doctor shall not provide any premises, instruments, substances or knowledge to facilitate the practice of torture or other forms of cruel, inhuman or degrading treatment or to diminish the ability of the victim to resist such treatment.

3. The doctor shall not be present during any procedure during which torture or other forms of cruel, inhuman or degrading treatment is used or threatened.

4. A doctor must have complete clinical independence in deciding upon the care of a person for whom he or she is medically responsible. The doctor's fundamental role is to alleviate the distress of his or her fellow men, and no motive, whether personal, collective or political shall prevail against this higher purpose.

5. Where a prisoner refuses nourishment and is considered by the doctor as capable of forming an unimpaired and rational judgment concerning the consequences of such a voluntary refusal of nourishment, he or she shall not be fed artificially. The decision as to the capacity of the prisoner to form such a judgment should be confirmed by at least one other independent doctor. The consequences of the refusal of nourishment shall be explained by the doctor to the prisoner.

6. The World Medical Association will support, and should encourage the international community, the national medical associations and fellow doctors, to support the doctor and his or her family in the face of threats or reprisals resulting from a refusal to condone the use of torture or other forms of cruel, inhuman or degrading treatment.

Resolution on Physician Participation in Capital Punishment
(World Medical Association, 1981)

Following concern about the introduction of an execution method (lethal injection) which threatened to involve doctors directly in the process of execution, the WMA Secretary-General issued a press statement opposing any involvement of doctors in capital punishment. The 34th Assembly of the WMA, meeting in Lisbon some weeks after the issuing of the press statement, endorsed the Secretary-General's statement in the following terms:

Resolution on Physician Participation in Capital Punishment

Resolved, that the assembly of the World Medical Association endorses the action of the Secretary-General in issuing the attached press release on behalf of the World Medical Association condemning physician participation in capital punishment.

Further resolved, that it is unethical for physicians to participate in capital punishment, although this does not preclude physicians certifying death.

Further Resolved, that the Medical Ethics Committee keep this matter under active consideration.

****

Secretary-General's Press Release   September 11, 1981

The first capital punishment by intravenous injection of lethal dose of drugs was decided to be carried out next week by the court of the State of Oklahoma, USA.

Regardless of the method of capital punishment a state imposes, no physician should be required to be an active participant. Physicians are dedicated to preserving life.

Acting as an executioner is not the practice of medicine, and physician services are not required to carry out capital punishment even if the methodology utilizes pharmacological agents or equipment that might otherwise be used in the practice of medicine.

A physician's only role would be to certify death once the State had carried out the capital punishment.

Declaration of Malta on Hunger Strikers

(World Medical Assembly, 1991, 1992)

A Declaration on Hunger Strikers, which sets guidelines for doctors responsible for the health of hunger strikers, was adopted by the 43rd World Medical Assembly in Malta in November 1991. The text was editorially revised at the 44th Assembly of the WMA meeting in Marbella, Spain, in September 1992. The text of the Declaration is as follows.

Declaration of Malta on Hunger Strikers

Preamble

1. The doctor treating hunger strikers is faced with the following conflicting values:

1.1 There is a moral obligation on every human being to respect the sanctity of life. This is especially evident in the case of a doctor, who exercises his skills to save life and also acts in the best interests of his patients (Beneficence).

1.2 It is the duty of the doctor to respect the autonomy which the patient has over his person. A doctor requires informed consent from his patients before applying any of his skills to assist them, unless emergency circumstances have arisen in which case the doctor has to act in what is perceived to be the patient's best interests.

2. This conflict is apparent where a hunger striker who has issued clear instructions not to be resuscitated lapses into a coma and is about to die. Moral obligation urges the doctor to resuscitate the patient even though it is against the patient's wishes. On the other hand, duty urges the doctor to respect the autonomy of the patient.

2.1 Ruling in favour of intervention may undermine the autonomy which the patient has over himself.

2.2 Ruling in favour of non-intervention may result in a doctor having to face the tragedy of an avoidable death.

3. A doctor/patient relationship is said to be in existence whenever a doctor is duty bound, by virtue of his obligation to the patient, to apply his skills to any person, be it in the form of advice or treatment.

This relationship can exist in spite of the fact that the patient might not consent to certain forms of treatment or intervention.

Once the doctor agrees to attend to a hunger striker, that person becomes the doctor's patient. This has all the implication and responsibilities inherent in the doctor/patient relationship, including consent and confidentiality.

4. The ultimate decision on intervention or non-intervention should be left with the individual doctor without the intervention of third parties whose primary interest is not the patient's welfare. However, the doctor should clearly state to the patient whether or not he is able to accept the patient's decision to refuse treatment or, in case of coma, artificial feeding, thereby risking death. It the doctor cannot accept the patient's decision to refuse such aid, the patient would then be entitled to be attended by another physician.

Guidelines for the Management of Hunger Strikers

Since the medical profession considers the principle of sanctity of life to be fundamental to its practice, the following practical guidelines are recommended for doctors who treat hunger strikers:

1. Definition

A hunger striker is a mentally competent person who has indicated that he has decided to embark on a hunger strike and has refused to take food and/or fluids for a significant interval.

2. Ethical Behaviour

2.1 A doctor should acquire a detailed medical history of the patient where possible.

2.2 A doctor should carry out a thorough examination of the patient at the onset of the hunger strike.

2.3 Doctors or other health care personnel may not apply undue pressure of any sort on the hunger striker to suspend the strike. Treatment or care of the hunger striker must not be conditional upon him suspending his hunger strike.

2.4 The hunger striker must be professionally informed by the doctor of the clinical consequences of a hunger strike, and of any specific danger to his own particular case. An informed decision can only be made on the basis of clear communication. An interpreter should be used if indicated.

2.5 Should a hunger striker wish to have a second medical opinion, this should be granted. Should a hunger striker prefer his treatment to be continued by the second doctor, this should be permitted. In the case of the hunger striker being a prisoner, this should be permitted by arrangement and consultation with the appointed prison doctor.

2.6 Treating infections or advising the patient to increase his oral intake of fluid (or accept intravenous saline solutions) is often acceptable to a hunger striker. A refusal to accept such intervention must not prejudice any other aspect of the patient's health care. Any treatment administered to the patient must be with his approval.

3. Clear Instructions

The doctor should ascertain on a daily basis whether or not the patient wishes to continue with his hunger strike. The doctor should also ascertain on a daily basis what the patient's wishes are with regard to treatment should he become unable to make an informed decision. These findings must be recorded in the doctor's personal medical records and kept confidential.

4. Artificial Feeding

When the hunger striker has become confused and is therefore unable to make an unimpaired decision or has lapsed into a coma, the doctor shall be free to make the decision for his patient as to further treatment which he considers to be in the best interest of that patient, always taking into account the decision he has arrived at during his preceding care of the patient during his hunger strike, and reaffirming article 4 of the preamble of this Declaration.

5. Coercion

Hunger strikers should be protected from coercive participation. This may require removal from the presence of fellow strikers.

6. Family

The doctor has a responsibility to inform the family of the patient that the patient has embarked on a hunger strike, unless this is specifically prohibited by the patient.

Statements by
professional associations

Psychiatrists

- Declaration of Hawaii

- Declaration on the participation of psychiatrists
in the death penalty

The Declaration of Hawaii

(World Psychiatric Association, 1977, 1983)

*In early 1976 work commenced on the drafting of an international code of
ethics for psychiatrists which was subsequently adopted in 1977 at the VIth
World Congress of Psychiatry in Honolulu, Hawaii. At the same meeting the
WPA committed itself to receive and investigate allegations of the abuse of
psychiatry for political purposes; in 1979 the establishment of a Review
Committee was finalized and it first met in Paris in 1980.*

*The constitutional status of the Review Committee was changed at the VIIth
Congress in Vienna in July 1983 when it was made permanent and had its
remit widened.*

*Minor amendments to the text of the Declaration were agreed at the July
1983 Congress. The text, as amended, reads as follows.*

Declaration of Hawaii

*Ever since the dawn of culture, ethics has been an essential part of the
healing art. It is the view of the World Psychiatric Association that due to
conflicting loyalties and expectations of both physicians and patients in
contemporary society and the delicate nature of the therapist-patient
relationship, high ethical standards are especially important for those
involved in the science and practice of psychiatry as a medical specialty.
These guidelines have been delineated in order to promote close adherence
to those standards and to prevent misuse of psychiatric concepts, knowledge
and technology.*

*Since the psychiatrist is a member of society as well as a practitioner of
medicine, he or she must consider the ethical implications specific to
psychiatry as well as the ethical demands on all physicians and the societal
responsibility of every man and woman.*

*Even though ethical behaviour is based on the individual psychiatrist's
conscience and personal judgement, written guidelines are needed to clarify
the profession's ethical implications.*

*Therefore, the General Assembly of the World Psychiatric Association has
approved these ethical guidelines for psychiatrists, having in mind the great
differences in cultural backgrounds, and in legal, social and economic
conditions which exist in the various countries of the world. It should be
understood that the World Psychiatric Association views these guidelines to*

be minimal requirements for the ethical standards of the psychiatric profession.

1. The aim of psychiatry is to treat mental illness and to promote mental health. To the best of his or her ability, consistent with accepted scientific knowledge and ethical principles, the psychiatrist shall serve the best interests of the patient and be also concerned for the common good and a just allocation of health resources. To fulfil these aims requires continuous research and continual education of health care personnel, patients and the public.

2. Every psychiatrist should offer to the patient the best available therapy to his knowledge and if accepted must treat him or her with the solicitude and respect due to the dignity of all human beings. When the psychiatrist is responsible for treatment given by others he owes them competent supervision and education. Whenever there is a need, or whenever a reasonable request is forthcoming from the patient, the psychiatrist should seek the help of another colleague.

3. The psychiatrist aspires for a therapeutic relationship that is founded on mutual agreement. At its optimum it requires trust, confidentiality, co-operation and mutual responsibility. Such a relationship may not be possible to establish with some patients. In that case, contact should be established with a relative or other person close to the patient. If and when a relationship is established for purposes other than therapeutic, such as forensic psychiatry, its nature must be thoroughly explained to the person concerned.

4. The psychiatrist should inform the patient of the nature of the condition, therapeutic procedures, including possible alternatives, and of the possible outcome. This information must be offered in a considerate way and the patient must be given the opportunity to choose between appropriate and available methods.

5. No procedure shall be performed nor treatment given against or independent of a patient's own will, unless, because of mental illness, the patient cannot form a judgement as to what is in his or her best interests and without which treatment serious impairment is likely to occur to the patient or others.

6. As soon as the conditions for compulsory treatment no longer apply, the psychiatrist should release the patient from the compulsory nature of the treatment and if further therapy is necessary should obtain voluntary consent. The psychiatrist should inform the patient and/or relatives or meaningful

others, of the existence of mechanisms of appeal for the detention and for any other complaints related to his or her well-being.

7. The psychiatrist must never use his professional possibilities to violate the dignity or human rights of any individual or group and should never let inappropriate personal desires, feelings, prejudices or beliefs interfere with the treatment. The psychiatrist must on no account utilize the tools of his profession, once the absence of psychiatric illness has been established. If a patient or some third party demands actions contrary to scientific knowledge or ethical principles the psychiatrist must refuse to cooperate.

8. Whatever the psychiatrist has been told by the patient, or has noted during examination or treatment, must be kept confidential unless the patient relieves the psychiatrist from this obligation, or to prevent serious harm to self or others makes disclosure necessary. In these cases, however, the patient should be informed of the breach of confidentiality.

9. To increase and propagate psychiatric knowledge and skill requires participation of the patients. Informed consent must, however, be obtained before presenting a patient to a class and, if possible, also when a case history is released for scientific publication, whereby all reasonable measures must be taken to preserve the dignity and anonymity of the patient and to safeguard the personal reputation of the subject. The patient's participation must be voluntary, after full information has been given of the aim, procedures, risks and inconveniences of a research project and there must always be a reasonable relationship between calculated risks or inconveniences and the benefit of the study. In clinical research every subject must retain and exert all his rights as a patient. For children and other patients who cannot themselves give informed consent, this should be obtained from the legal next-of-kin. Every patient or research subject is free to withdraw for any reason at any time from any voluntary treatment and from any teaching or research program in which he or she participates. This withdrawal, as well as any refusal to enter a program, must never influence the psychiatrist's efforts to help the patient or subject.

10. The psychiatrist should stop all therapeutic, teaching or research programs that may evolve contrary to the principles of this Declaration.

Declaration on the participation of psychiatrists in the death penalty
(World Psychiatric Association, 1989)

The following declaration was adopted by the General Assembly of the World Psychiatric Association at its World Congress in Athens in October 1989.

Declaration on the participation of psychiatrists in the death penalty

Psychiatrists are physicians and adhere to the Hippocratic Oath "to practise for the good of their patients and never to do harm".

The World Psychiatric Association is an international association with 77 Member Societies.

Considering that the United Nations' Principles of Medical Ethics enjoins physicians - and thus psychiatrists - to refuse to enter into any relationship with a prisoner other than one directed at evaluation, protecting or improving their physical and mental health, and further,

Considering that the Declaration of Hawaii of the WPA resolves that the psychiatrist shall serve the best interests of the patient and treat every patient with the solicitude and respect due to the dignity of all human beings and that the psychiatrist must refuse to cooperate if some third party demands actions contrary to ethical principles,

Conscious that psychiatrists may be called on to participate in any action connected to executions,

Declares that the participation of psychiatrists in any such action is a violation of professional ethics.

Statements by professional associations

Nurses

- Role of the nurse in the care of detainees and prisoners

- Statement on the nurse's role in safeguarding human rights

- Position statement on nurses and torture

- Position statement on the death penalty and participation by nurses in executions

The Nurse's Role in the Care of Detainees and Prisoners
(International Council of Nurses, 1975)

At the meeting of the Council of National Representatives of the International Council of Nurses in Singapore in August 1975, a statement on the role of the nurse in the care of detainees and prisoners was adopted. The text, last reviewed in 1991, is as follows:

The Nurse's Role in the Care of Detainees and Prisoners

The International Council of Nurses (ICN) Code for Nurses[1] states that:

1. The fundamental responsibility of the nurse is fourfold: to promote health, to prevent illness, to restore health and to alleviate suffering.
2. The nurse's primary responsibility is to those people who require nursing care.
3. The nurse when acting in a professional capacity should at all times maintain standards of personal conduct which reflect credit upon the profession.
4. The nurse takes appropriate action to safeguard the individual when his care is endangered by a co-worker or any other person.

ICN has reaffirmed its support of the Geneva Conventions of 1949[2], and the additional protocols, which state that, in case of armed conflict of international as well as national character (i.e. internal disorders, civil wars, armed rebellions):

1. Members of the armed forces, prisoners and persons taking no active part in the hostilities
   a) shall be entitled to protection and care if wounded or sick,

---

[1]International Council of Nurses, Code for Nurses, Geneva, ICN, Adopted 1973, Reaffirmed in 1989.

[2]International Committee of the Red Cross, Rights and Duties of Nurses under the Geneva Convention of August 12, 1949, Geneva, ICRC, 1970.

24

b) shall be treated humanely, that is:

• they may not be subjected to physical mutilation or to medical or scientific experiments of any kind which are not justified by the medical, dental or hospital treatment of the prisoner concerned and carried out in his interest;

• they shall not be wilfully left without medical assistance and care, nor shall conditions exposing them to contagion or infection be created;

• they shall be treated humanely and cared for by the party in conflict in whose power they may be, without adverse distinction founded on sex, race, nationality, religion, political opinion or any other similar criteria.

2. The following acts are and shall remain prohibited at any time and in any place whatsoever with respect to the above mentioned persons:

a) violence to life and person, in particular murder of all kinds, mutilation, cruel treatment and torture;

b) outrages upon personal dignity, in particular humiliating and degrading treatment.

ICN has endorsed the United Nations Universal Declaration of Human Rights[3] and, hence, accepted that:

i) Everyone is entitled to all the rights and freedoms, set forth in this Declaration, without distinction of any kind, such as race, colour, sex, language, religion, political or other opinion, national or social origin, property, birth or other status (Art.2),

ii) No-one shall be subjected to torture or to cruel, inhuman or degrading treatment or punishment (Art.5).

In relation to detainees and prisoners of conscience, interrogation procedures are increasingly being employed resulting in ill effects, often permanent, on the person's mental and physical health. ICN condemns the use of all such procedures harmful to the mental and physical health of prisoners and detainees.

Nurses having knowledge of physical or mental ill-treatment of detainees and prisoners must take appropriate action including reporting the matter to appropriate national and/or international bodies.

---

[3]United Nations Universal Declaration of Human Rights, United Nations, Adopted 10 December 1948.

Nurses employed in prison health services do not assume functions of prison security personnel, such as body search for prison security reasons.

Nurses participate in clinical research carried out on prisoners only if the freely given consent of the patient has been secured after a complete explanation and understanding by the patient of the nature and risk of the research.

The nurse's first responsibility is towards the patients, notwithstanding considerations of national security and interest.

The Nurse's Role
in Safeguarding Human Rights
(International Council of Nurses, 1983)

Responding to requests from national associations for guidance on the protection of human rights of both nurses and those for whom they care, the Council of Nurses Representatives of the International Council of Nurses adopted a statement at its meeting in Brasilia in June 1983. The statement, last reviewed in 1991, is given below:

The Nurse's Role in Safeguarding Human Rights

The current world situation is such that a nurse may become involved in innumerable circumstances requiring action on her/his part to safeguard human rights. Nurses are accountable for their own professional actions and therefore must know what is expected of them in such situations.

Conflict situations have increased in number and include internal political upheaval, strife, or international war. Even the nature of war is changing. Increasingly nurses find themselves having to act or respond to complex situations with no clear-cut solution.

Changes in the field of communications also have increased the awareness and sensitivity of all groups to conflict situations.

The need for nursing actions to safeguard human rights is not restricted to times of political upheaval and war. It can also arise in prisons or in the normal work situation of any nurse where abuse of patients, nurses or others is witnessed or suspected. Nurses have a responsibility in these situations to take action to safeguard the rights of those involved. Physical and/or mental abuse, over or under treatment are equally of concern to the nurse. There may be pressures applied to use one's knowledge and skills in ways that are not beneficial to patients or others.

Scientific discoveries have brought about more sophisticated forms of torture and methods of resuscitation so that victims of torture can be kept alive for repeated sessions. It is in such circumstances that nurses must know what actions they must take, as in no way can they participate in such torture or torture techniques.

Nurses have individual responsibility but they often can be more effective if they approach human rights issues as a group. The national nurses' associations (NNAs) need to ensure that their structure provides a realistic mechanism through which nurses can seek confidential advice, counsel, support and assistance in dealing with these difficult situations. Verification of the facts reported will be an important first step in any particular case.

At times it will be appropriate for the NNA to speak on behalf of the nurses involved or to negotiate for them. It is essential that confidentiality be maintained. In rare cases the personal judgement of the nurse may indicate that approaching the association is not the appropriate action.

The nurse initiating the actions requires knowledge of human rights, moral courage, an adequate plan of action and a commitment and determination to see that the necessary follow-up does occur. Personal risk is a factor that has to be considered and each person must use her/his best judgement in the situation.

Rights of those in need of care

- Health care is a right for all individuals. Everyone should have access to health care regardless of financial, political, geographic, racial or religious considerations. The nurse should seek to ensure such impartial treatment.

- Nurses must ensure that adequate treatment is provided — within available resources — and in accord with nursing ethics (ICN Code for Nurses[1]) to all those in need of care.

- A patient/prisoner has the right to refuse to eat or to refuse treatments. The nurse may need to verify that the patient/prisoner understands the implications of such action but she should not participate in the administration of food or medications to such patients.

Rights and duties of nurses

- When considering the rights and duties of nursing personnel it needs to be remembered that both action and lack of action can have a detrimental effect and that the nursing personnel must be considered accountable on both counts.

- Nurses have a right to practise within the code of ethics and nursing legislation of the country in which they practise. Personal safety - freedom from abuse, threats, or intimidation - are the rights of every nurse.

---

[1]International Council of Nurses, Code for Nurses, Geneva, ICN, Adopted 1973, Reaffirmed in 1989.

- National nurses' associations have a responsibility to participate in the development of health and social legislation relative to patients' rights and all related topics.

- It is a duty to have informed consent of patients when research is done on them and when they receive treatments such as blood transfusions, anaesthesia, grafts, etc. Such informed consent is a patient's right and must be ensured.

Nurses and Torture
(International Council of Nurses, 1989)

A statement on nurses and torture was adopted at the meeting of the Council of National Representatives of the International Council of Nurses in Seoul in May 1989. The text, last reviewed in 1991, is given below.

Nurses and Torture

Violations of human rights have become more pervasive and scientific discoveries have brought about more sophisticated forms of torture and methods of resuscitation.

Although nurses may not voluntarily participate in any form of physical or psychological torture, they must know what is expected of them and what action they must take to safeguard human rights.[1]

Nurses need to know that, although the apparent motive for much of the treatment during and after torture in the protection of the victim, it is often carried out more as protection of the torturers.

The nurse may be called upon to act alone or to assist in the following situations:

• To perform physical examinations on suspects before they are subjected to forms of interrogation, which might include torture;

• to attend a torture session in order to intervene when the victim's life is in danger;

• To treat the direct physical effects of torture, so that later the interrogation can be continued.[2]

The nurse's primary responsibility is to those people who require nursing care. If the victim of cruel, wanton, degrading or any other inhuman procedure or treatment (in the independent opinion of the nurse) requires

---

[1]International Council of Nurses. The Nurse's Role in Safe-guarding Human Rights. Position statement, adopted 1983, reviewed 1991.

[2]Amnesty International. *Codes of Professional Ethics.* 2nd Edition. London: Amnesty International Publications, 1984.

nursing care, then no motive should prevail against the nurse giving such care to the highest standard possible.

The national nurses associations (NNAs) need to ensure that their structure provides a realistic mechanism through which nurses can seek confidential advice, counsel, support and assistance in dealing with these difficult situations. Verification of the facts reported will be an important first step in any particular case.

The Responsibility of the Nurse

The nurse shall not countenance, condone or voluntarily participate in:

- Any deliberate, systematic or wanton infliction of physical or mental suffering or any other form of cruel, inhuman or degrading procedure by one or more persons acting alone or on the orders of any authority, to force another person to yield information, to make a confession or for any other reason

- Any treatment which denies to any person the respect which is his/her due as a human being.

Death Penalty and Participation by Nurses in Executions

(International Council of Nurses, 1989)

The International Council of Nurses adopted the following statement at its meeting of the Council of National Representatives in Seoul in May 1989. The text was last reviewed in 1991.

Death Penalty and Participation by Nurses in Executions

The ICN Code for Nurses[1] states that ... *inherent in nursing is respect for life, dignity and the rights of man* and further states that ... *the fundamental responsibility of the nurse is fourfold: to promote health, to prevent illness, to restore health and to alleviate suffering.*

The International Council of Nurses (ICN) has always fully supported the United Nations Declaration of Human Rights[2] in which is established the right of the individual to life; and the right of the individual not to be subject to cruel, inhuman or degrading treatment (a right also upheld in the two ICN position statements: The nurse's role in safeguarding human rights[3] and The nurse's role in the care of detainees and prisoners[4].

Although many countries have abolished the death penalty, it still remains a legalized form of punishment in some countries. In a number of these countries, there has been an alarming increase in prisoners sentenced to death.

---

[1]International Council of Nurses, Code for Nurses, Geneva, ICN, Adopted 1973, Reaffirmed 1989.

[2]United Nations, Universal Declaration of Human Rights, United Nations, Adopted 10 December 1948.

[3]International Council of Nurses, The Nurse's Role in Safeguarding Human Rights, Position Statement, Adopted 1983, Reviewed 1991.

[4]International Council of Nurses, The Nurse's Role in the Care of Detainees and Prisoners, Position Statement, Adopted 1975, Reviewed 1985 and 1991.

All efforts to regulate and humanize this form of punishment have thus far only created a vastly complicated, contradictory and ineffective legal and ethical morass.

ICN recognizes the responsibility of the nurse to a prisoner sentenced to death by the state continues until the actual execution procedure is initiated; and considers participation by nurses, either directly or indirectly, in the immediate preparation for and the carrying out of state authorized executions to be a violation of nursing's ethical code. ICN thus calls on national nurses' associations to work for the abolishment of the death penalty in all countries still practising this form of punishment.

Statements by
professional associations

Psychologists

- Statement by the International Union
of Psychological Science

Statement by the International Union
of Psychological Science
(July 1976)

In July 1976, the Assembly of the International Union of Psychological Science unanimously approved the statement of the Executive Committee of the International Union of Psychological Science made in July 1974. The text is as follows:

Statement of the IUPsyS

The International Union of Psychological Science

which includes national psychological societies of 51 nations from all over the world;

which thus speaks in the name of over 130,000 professional psychologists who, because the subject of their science is behaviour, are particularly concerned with any acts by which individuals in a systematic and deliberate way infringe upon the inviolable rights of human beings, regardless of race, religion or ideology, these rights being guaranteed by the Charter of the United Nations;

and which is concerned with the strict observance of professional standards of ethics in the practice of psychology;

therefore makes the following declarations:

It proclaims that no psychologist, in the exercise of his or her professional functions, should accept instructions or motivations that are inspired by considerations that are foreign to the profession;

It protests solemnly against any use of scientific data or of professional methods of psychology that impair the above mentioned rights;

It formally condemns any collaboration by psychologists - whether actively or passively, directly or indirectly - with the above mentioned abuses, and it urges its members to oppose any abuses of this sort;

It requests each member-society to make certain that it has enacted a code of ethics and to take those actions required by its code against any member guilty of such abuses against human rights;

It declares that the Executive Committee of IUPsyS is ready to support, with all means at its disposal, any action undertaken by a member-society in order to carry out the terms of the present resolution;

It recalls the following statement made by its Executive Committee on July 12 1974: "The Executive Committee wishes to make clear that the International Union of Psychological Science denounces vigorously all practices that are contrary to the high level of morality that must regulate the scientific and professional roles assumed by psychologists in modern society."

It welcomes the United Nations resolution, adopted by the General Assembly (Third Committee: A/10408; 243rd plenary meeting, 9 December 1975) on the protection of all persons from being subjected to Inhuman Treatment[1].

---

[1]Subsequently adopted as the United Nations Declaration Against Torture [AI footnote].

Statements by
professional associations

Prison health care professionals

- Oath of Athens

The Oath of Athens
(International Council of Prison Medical Services, 1979)

The International Council of Prison Medical Services was established in 1977. The first World Congress of Prison Medicine, which took place in Dijon in November 1978, was held under its auspices. The Oath of Athens was unanimously approved by the International Council the following year.

The Oath of Athens

We, the health professionals who are working in prison settings, meeting in Athens on September 10, 1979, hereby pledge, in keeping with the spirit of the Oath of Hippocrates, that we shall endeavour to provide the best possible health care for those who are incarcerated in prisons for whatever reasons, without prejudice and within our respective professional ethics.

We recognize the right of the incarcerated individuals to receive the best possible health care.

We undertake

1. To abstain from authorizing or approving any physical punishment.

2. To abstain from participating in any form of torture.

3. Not to engage in any form of human experimentation amongst incarcerated individuals without their informed consent.

4. To respect the confidentiality of any information obtained in the course of our professional relationships with incarcerated patients.

5. That our medical judgements be based on the needs of our patients and take priority over any non-medical matters.

The Hippocratic Oath

The Hippocratic Oath

(5th Century BC)

It is not certain that the Hippocratic Oath was written by Hippocrates but it was probably written during his lifetime. The earliest surviving references to this Oath date from the 1st century AD. These suggested that the Oath was seen as an ideal rather than a norm and it was not until the 4th century that it was an obligatory requirement for the doctor to take the oath before practising.

The Hippocratic Oath

I swear by Apollo Physician and Asclepius and Hygieia and Panaceia and all the gods and goddesses, making them my witnesses, that I will fulfil according to my ability and judgement this oath and this covenant:

To hold him who has taught me this art as equal to my parents and to live my life in partnership with him, and if he is in need of money to give him a share of mine, and to regard his offspring as equal to my brothers in male lineage and to teach them this art - if they desire to learn it - without fee and covenant; to give a share of precepts and oral instruction and all the other learning to my sons and to the sons of him who has instructed me and to pupils who have signed the covenant and have taken an oath according to the medical law, but to no one else.

I will apply dietetic measures for the benefit of the sick according to my ability and judgement; I will keep them from harm and injustice.

I will neither give a deadly drug to anybody if asked for it, nor will I make a suggestion to this effect. Similarly I will not give to a woman an abortive remedy. In purity and holiness I will guard my life and my art.

I will not use the knife, not even on sufferers from stone, but will withdraw in favour of such men as are engaged in this work.

Whatever houses I may visit, I will come for the benefit of the sick, remaining free of all intentional injustice, of all mischief and in particular of sexual relations with both female and male persons, be they free or slaves.

What I may see or hear in the course of the treatment or even outside of the treatment in regard to the life of men, which on no account one must spread abroad, I will keep to myself holding such things shameful to be spoken about.

If I fulfil this oath and do not violate it, may it be granted to me to enjoy life and art, being honoured with fame among all men for all time to come; if I transgress it and swear falsely, may the opposite of all this be my lot.

*Common article 3 of the
Geneva Conventions*

Common Article 3 of the Geneva Conventions
(Geneva Conventions, 1949)

International humanitarian law as defined today is largely contained in the four Geneva Conventions of 1949 applicable during times of international armed conflict. The Conventions prescribe that individuals not participating directly in hostilities and those who are wounded, sick or placed hors de combat *be cared for without discrimination. Apart from specific articles in the conventions prohibiting ill-treatment, common article 3 — found identically in all four Conventions — establishes minimum rules for the protection of victims of "armed conflict not of an international character". The text of this article is given below.*

(The full text of the Geneva Conventions and additional protocols is given in: The Geneva Conventions of August 12, 1949, *Geneva: ICRC, 245 pp, undated, and in* Protocols Additional to the Geneva Conventions of 12 August 1949, *Geneva: ICRC, 1977, 136pp.)*

Common Article 3 of the Geneva Conventions

In the case of armed conflict not of an international character occurring in the territory of one of the High Contracting Parties, each Party to the conflict shall be bound to apply, as a minimum, the following provisions:

(1) Persons taking no active part in the hostilities, including members of armed forces who have laid down their arms and those placed *hors de combat* by sickness, wounds, detention, or any other cause, shall in all circumstances be treated humanely, without any adverse distinction founded on race, colour, religion or faith, sex, birth or wealth, or any other similar criteria.

To this end, the following acts are and shall remain prohibited at any time and in any place whatsoever with respect to the above-mentioned persons:

(a) violence to life and person, in particular murder of all kinds, mutilation, cruel treatment and torture;
(b) taking of hostages;
(c) outrages upon personal dignity, in particular humiliating and degrading treatment;
(d) the passing of sentences and the carrying out of executions without previous judgment pronounced by a regularly constituted court, affording

all the judicial guarantees which are recognized as indispensable by civilized peoples.

(2) The wounded and sick shall be collected and cared for.

An impartial humanitarian body, such as the International Committee of the Red Cross, may offer its services to the Parties to the conflict.

The Parties to the conflict should further endeavour to bring into force, by means of special agreements, all or part of the other provisions of the present Convention.

The application of the preceding provisions shall not affect the legal status of the Parties to the conflict.

47

United Nations Declarations Principles and Conventions

- Principles of medical ethics relevant to the role of health personnel, particularly physicians, in the protection of prisoners and detainees against torture and other cruel, inhuman or degrading treatment or punishment

- Convention against torture and other cruel, inhuman or degrading treatment or punishment

- Principles on the effective prevention and investigation of extra-legal, arbitrary and summary executions

- Principles for the protection of persons with mental illness and for the improvement of mental health care

- Body of principles for the protection of all persons under any form of detention or imprisonment

- Standard minimum rules for the treatment of prisoners and procedures for the effective implementation of the standard minimum rules

Principles of Medical Ethics
(United Nations, 1982)

The principles are elaborated within the text of the Resolution 37/194, adopted by the United Nations General Assembly, 18 December 1982.

Principles of medical ethics relevant to the role of health personnel, particularly physicians, in the protection of prisoners and detainees against torture and other cruel, inhuman or degrading treatment or punishment

The General Assembly...[1]

Desirous of setting further standards in this field which ought to be implemented by health personnel, particularly physicians, and by government officials,

1. Adopts the Principles of Medical Ethics relevant to the role of health personnel, particularly physicians, in the protection of prisoners and detainees against torture and other cruel, inhuman or degrading treatment or punishment set forth in the annex to the present resolution;

2. Calls upon all Governments to give the Principles of Medical Ethics, together with the present resolution, the widest possible distribution, in particular among medical and paramedical associations and institutions of detention or imprisonment in an official language of the state.

3. Invites all relevant inter-governmental organizations, in particular the World Health Organization, and non-governmental organizations concerned to bring the Principles of Medical Ethics to the attention of the widest possible group of individuals, especially those active in the medical and paramedical field.

---

[1]The preamble to the resolution has been edited by AI. The full document is available from the UN Information Offices, Ref: A/RES/37/194.

Principles of medical ethics relevant to the role of health personnel, particularly physicians, in the protection of prisoners and detainees against torture and other cruel, inhuman or degrading treatment or punishment

Principle 1

Health personnel, particularly physicians, charged with the medical care of prisoners and detainees have the duty to provide them with protection of their physical and mental health and treatment of disease of the same quality and standard as is afforded to those who are not imprisoned or detained.

Principle 2

It is a gross contravention of medical ethics, as well as an offence under applicable international instruments, for health personnel, particularly physicians, to engage, actively or passively, in acts which constitute participation in, complicity in, incitement to or attempts to commit torture or other cruel, inhuman or degrading treatment or punishment.[1]

---

[1]See the Declaration on the Protection of All Persons from Being Subjected to Torture and Other Cruel, Inhuman or Degrading Treatment or Punishment (General Assembly Resolution 3452 (XXX), annex), article 1 of which states:
"1. For the purpose of this Declaration, torture means any act by which severe pain or suffering, whether physical or mental, is intentionally inflicted by or at the instigation of a public official on a person for such purposes as obtaining from him or a third person information or confession, punishing him for an act he has committed or is suspected of having committed, or intimidating him or other persons. It does not include pain or suffering arising only from, inherent or incidental to, lawful sanctions to the extent consistent with the Standard Minimum Rules for the Treatment of Prisoners.
2. Torture constitutes an aggravated and deliberate form of cruel, inhuman or degrading treatment or punishment."
Article 7 of the Declaration states:
"Each state shall ensure that all acts of torture as defined in article 1 are offences under its criminal law. The same shall apply in regard to acts which constitute participation in, complicity in, incitement to or an attempt to commit torture."

51

Principle 3

It is a contravention of medical ethics for health personnel, particularly physicians, to be involved in any professional relationship with prisoners or detainees the purpose of which is not to solely evaluate, protect or improve their physical and mental health.

Principle 4

It is a contravention of medical ethics for health personnel, particularly physicians:

a) To apply their knowledge and skills in order to assist in the interrogation of prisoners and detainees in a manner that may adversely affect the physical or mental health or condition of such prisoners or detainees and which is not in accordance with the relevant international instruments[2];

b) To certify, or to participate in the certification of, the fitness of prisoners or detainees for any form of treatment or punishment that may adversely affect their physical or mental health and which is not in accordance with the relevant international instruments, or to participate in any way in the infliction of any such treatment or punishment which is not in accordance with the relevant international instruments.

Principle 5

It is a contravention of medical ethics for health personnel, particularly physicians, to participate in any procedure for restraining a prisoner or detainee unless such a procedure is determined in accordance with purely medical criteria as being necessary for the protection of the physical or mental health or the safety of the prisoner or detainee himself, of his

---

[2]Particularly the Universal Declaration of Human Rights (General Assembly Resolution 217 A (III)), the International Covenants on Human Rights (General Assembly Resolution 2200 A (XXI), annex), the Declaration on the Protection of all Persons from Being Subjected to Torture and Other Cruel, Inhuman or Degrading Treatment or Punishment (General Assembly Resolution 3452 (XXX), annex) and the Standard Minimum Rules for the Treatment of Prisoners (First United Nations Congress on the Prevention of Crime and the Treatment of Offenders: report by the Secretariat (United Nations publication, Sales No. 1956.IV.4), annex IA).

fellow prisoners or detainees, or of his guardians, and presents no hazard to his physical or mental health.

Principle 6

There may be no derogation from the foregoing principles on any grounds whatsoever, including public emergency.

Convention against Torture and Other Cruel, Inhuman or Degrading Treatment or Punishment

(United Nations, 1984)

The Convention against Torture was adopted by consensus by the United Nations General Assembly by resolution 39/46 of 10 December 1984 and came into force on 26 June 1987. It provides for a Committee against Torture comprised of ten elected individuals. This committee is empowered to examine reports of torture from any country party to the Convention and will seek the full cooperation of the State party concerned in any inquiry which is instituted.

Extracts are given here from Part 1 and Part 2 of the Convention. Part 3 is omitted. Part 1 deals with the obligations of state parties to outlaw torture and Part 2 with the remit and procedures of the Committee. The full document is available from the United Nations information offices and is published in "Human Rights: A Compilation of International Instruments", Geneva: United Nations, 1988.

Convention against Torture and Other Cruel, Inhuman or Degrading Treatment or Punishment

Part 1

Article 1

1. For the purposes of this Convention, the term "torture" means any act by which severe pain or suffering, whether physical or mental, is intentionally inflicted on a person for such purposes as obtaining from him or a third person information or a confession, punishing him for an act he or a third person has committed or is suspected of having committed, or intimidating or coercing him or a third person, or for any reason based on discrimination of any kind, when such pain or suffering is inflicted by or at the instigation of or with the consent or acquiescence of a public official or other person acting in an official capacity. It does not include pain or suffering arising only from, inherent in, or incidental to lawful sanctions.

2. This article is without prejudice to any international instrument or national legislation which does or may contain provisions of wider application.

Article 2

1. Each State Party shall take effective legislative, administrative, judicial or other measures to prevent acts of torture in any territory under its jurisdiction.

2. No exceptional circumstances whatsoever, whether a state of war or a threat of war, internal political instability or any other public emergency, may be invoked as a justification of torture.

3. An order from a superior officer or a public authority may not be invoked as a justification of torture.

Article 3

1. No State Party shall expel, return (*"refouler"*) or extradite a person to another State where there are substantial grounds for believing that he would be in danger of being subjected to torture.

2. For the purpose of determining whether there are such grounds, the competent authorities shall take into account all relevant considerations including, where applicable, the existence in the State concerned of a consistent pattern of gross, flagrant or mass violations of human rights.

Article 4

1. Each State Party shall ensure that all acts of torture are offenses under its criminal law. The same shall apply to an attempt to commit torture and to an act by any person which constitutes complicity or participation in torture.

2. Each State Party shall make these offenses punishable by appropriate penalties which take into account their grave nature. [...]

Article 10

1. Each State Party shall ensure that education and information regarding the prohibition against torture are fully included in the training of law enforcement personnel, civil or military, medical personnel, public officials and other persons who may be involved in the custody, interrogation or treatment of any individual subjected to any form of arrest, detention or imprisonment.

2. Each State Party shall include this prohibition in the rules or instructions issued in regard to the duties and functions of any such persons. [...]

Article 14

1. Each State Party shall ensure in its legal system that the victim of an act of torture obtains redress and has an enforceable right to fair and adequate compensation, including the means for as full rehabilitation as possible. In the event of the death of the victim as a result of an act of torture, his dependants shall be entitled to compensation.

2. Nothing in this article shall affect any right of the victim or other persons to compensation which may exist under national law.

Article 15

Each State Party shall ensure that any statement which is established to have been made as a result of torture shall not be invoked as evidence in any proceedings, except against a person accused of torture as evidence that the statement was made. [...]

Part II

Article 17

1. There shall be established a Committee against Torture (hereinafter referred to as the Committee) which shall carry out the functions hereinafter provided. The Committee shall consist of ten experts of high moral standing and recognized competence in the field of human rights, who shall serve in their personal capacity. The experts shall be elected by the States Parties, consideration being given to equitable geographical distribution and to the usefulness of the participation of some persons having legal experience. [...]

Article 19

1. The States Parties shall submit to the Committee, through the Secretary-General of the United Nations, reports on the measures they have taken to give effect to their undertakings under this Convention, within one year after the entry into force of the Convention for the State Party concerned. Thereafter the States Parties shall submit supplementary reports every four years on any new measures taken and such other reports as the Committee may request.

2. The Secretary-General of the United Nations shall transmit the reports to all States Parties.

3. Each report shall be considered by the Committee which may make such general comments on the report as it may consider appropriate and shall forward these to the State Party concerned. That State Party may respond with any observations it chooses to the Committee.

4. The Committee may, at its discretion, decide to include any comments made by it in accordance with paragraph 3 of this article, together with the observations thereon received from the State Party concerned, in its annual report made in accordance with article 24. If so requested by the State Party concerned, the Committee may also include a copy of the report submitted under paragraph 1 of this article.

Article 20

1. If the Committee receives reliable information which appears to it to contain well-founded indications that torture is being systematically practised in the territory of a State Party, the Committee shall invite that State Party to cooperate in the examination of the information and to this end to submit observations with regard to the information concerned.

2. Taking into account any observations which may have been submitted by the State Party concerned, as well as any other relevant information available to it, the Committee may, if it decides that this is warranted, designate one or more of its members to make a confidential inquiry and to report to the Committee urgently.

3. If an inquiry is made in accordance with paragraph 2 of this article, the Committee shall seek the cooperation of the State Party concerned. In agreement with that State Party, such an inquiry may include a visit to its territory.

4. After examining the findings of its member or members submitted in accordance with paragraph 2 of this article, the Committee shall transmit these findings to the State Party concerned together with any comments or suggestions which seem appropriate in view of the situation.

5. All the proceedings of the Committee referred to in paragraphs 1 to 4 of this article shall be confidential and at all stages of the proceedings the cooperation of the State Party shall be sought. After such proceedings have been completed with regard to an inquiry made in accordance with paragraph 2, the Committee may, after consultations with the State Party concerned,

decide to include a summary account of the results of the proceedings in its annual report made in accordance with article 24. [...]

Article 24

The Committee shall submit an annual report on its activities under this Convention to the States Parties and to the General Assembly of the United Nations.

Principles on the Effective Prevention and Investigation of Extra-legal, Arbitrary and Summary Executions

(United Nations, May 1989)

Resolution 1989/65 on the prevention of extrajudicial executions and adequate investigation of such executions was adopted by the United Nations' Economic and Social Council on 24 May 1989 and endorsed by the UN General Assembly in December 1989. The preamble to the resolution is not given here.

Principles on the Effective Prevention and Investigation of Extra-legal, Arbitrary and Summary Executions

Prevention

1. Governments shall prohibit by law all extra-legal, arbitrary and summary executions and shall ensure that any such executions are recognized as offences under their criminal laws, and are punishable by appropriate penalties which take into account the seriousness of such offences. Exceptional circumstances including a state of war or threat of war, internal political instability or any other public emergency may not be invoked as a justification of such executions. Such executions shall not be carried out under any circumstances including, but not limited to, situations of internal armed conflict, excessive or illegal use of force by a public official or other person acting in an official capacity or a person acting at the instigation, or with the consent or acquiescence of such person, and situations in which deaths occur in custody. This prohibition shall prevail over decrees issued by governmental authority.

2. In order to prevent extra-legal, arbitrary and summary executions, Governments shall ensure strict control, including a clear chain of command over all officials responsible for the apprehension, arrest, detention, custody and imprisonment as well as those officials authorized by law to use force and firearms.

3. Governments shall prohibit orders from superior officers or public authorities authorizing or inciting other persons to carry out any such extra-legal, arbitrary or summary executions. All persons shall have the right and the duty to defy such orders. Training of law enforcement officials shall emphasize the above provisions.

4. Effective protection through judicial or other means shall be guaranteed to individuals and groups who are in danger of extra-legal, arbitrary or summary executions, including those who receive death threats.

5. No one shall be involuntarily returned or extradited to a country where there are substantial grounds for believing that he or she may become a victim of extra-legal, arbitrary or summary execution in that country.

6. Governments shall ensure that persons deprived of their liberty are held in officially recognized places of custody, and that accurate information on their custody and whereabouts, including transfers, is made promptly available to their relatives and lawyer or other persons of confidence.

7. Qualified inspectors, including medical personnel, or an equivalent independent authority, shall conduct inspections in places of custody on a regular basis, and be empowered to undertake unannounced inspections on their own initiative, with full guarantees of independence in the exercise of this function. The inspectors shall have unrestricted access to all persons in such places of custody, as well as to all their records.

8. Government shall make every effort to prevent extra-legal, arbitrary and summary executions through measures such as diplomatic intercession, improved access of complainants to intergovernmental and judicial bodies, and public denunciation. Intergovernmental mechanisms shall be used to investigate reports of any such executions and to take effective action against such practice. Governments, including those of countries where extra-legal, arbitrary and summary executions are reasonably suspected to occur, shall cooperate fully in international investigations on the subject.

Investigation

9. There shall be a thorough, prompt and impartial investigation of all suspected cases of extra-legal, arbitrary and summary executions, including cases where complaints by relatives or other reliable reports suggest unnatural death in the above circumstances. Governments shall maintain investigative offices and procedures to undertake such inquiries. The purpose of the investigation shall be to determine the cause, manner and time of death, the

person responsible, and any pattern or practice which may have brought about that death. It shall include an adequate autopsy, collection and analysis of all physical and documentary evidence, and statements from witnesses. The investigation shall distinguish between natural death, accidental death, suicide and homicide.

10. The investigative authority shall have the power to obtain all the information necessary to the inquiry. Those persons conducting the investigation shall have at their disposal all the necessary budgetary and technical resources for effective investigation. They shall also have the authority to oblige officials allegedly involved in any such executions to appear and testify. The same shall apply to any witness. To this end, they shall be entitled to issue summons to witnesses including the officials allegedly involved and to demand the production of evidence.

11. In cases in which the established investigative procedures are inadequate because of lack of expertise or impartiality, because of the importance of the matter or because of the apparent existence of a pattern of abuse, and in cases where there are complaints from the family of the victim about these inadequacies or other substantial reasons, Governments shall pursue investigations through an independent commission of inquiry or similar procedure. Members of such a commission shall be chosen for their recognized impartiality, competence and independence as individuals. In particular, they shall be independent of any institution, agency or person that may be the subject of the inquiry. The commission shall have the authority to obtain all information necessary to the inquiry and shall conduct the inquiry as provided under these Principles.

12. The body of the deceased person shall not be disposed of until an adequate autopsy is conducted by a physician, who shall, if possible, be an expert in forensic pathology. Those conducting the autopsy shall have the right of access to all investigative data, to the place where the body was discovered, and to the place where the death is thought to have occurred. If the body has been buried and it later appears that an investigation is required, the body shall be promptly and competently exhumed for an autopsy. If skeletal remains are discovered, they should be carefully exhumed and studied according to systematic anthropological techniques.

13. The body of the deceased shall be available to those conducting the autopsy for a sufficient amount of time to enable a thorough investigation to be carried out. The autopsy shall, at a minimum, attempt to establish the identity of the deceased and the cause and manner of death. The time and

place of death shall also be determined to the extent possible. Detailed colour photographs of the deceased shall be included in the autopsy report in order to document and support the findings of the investigation. The autopsy report must describe any and all injuries to the deceased including any evidence of torture.

14. In order to ensure objective results, those conducting the autopsy must be able to function impartially and independently of any potentially implicated persons or organizations or entities.

15. Complainants, witnesses, those conducting the investigation and their families shall be protected from violence, threats of violence or any other form of intimidation. Those potentially implicated in extra-legal, arbitrary or summary executions shall be removed from any position of control or power, whether direct or indirect, over complainants, witnesses and their families, as well as over those conducting investigations.

16. Families of the deceased and their legal representatives shall be informed of, and have access to, any hearing as well as to all information relevant to the investigation, and shall be entitled to present other evidence. The family of the deceased shall have the right to insist that a medical or other qualified representative be present at the autopsy. When the identity of a deceased person has been determined, a notification of death shall be posted, and the family or relatives of the deceased immediately informed. The body of the deceased shall be returned to them upon completion of the investigation.

17. A written report shall be made within a reasonable period of time on the methods and findings of such investigations. The report shall be made public immediately and shall include the scope of the inquiry, procedures and methods used to evaluate evidence as well as conclusions and recommendations based on findings of fact and on applicable law. The report shall also describe in detail specific events that were found to have occurred, and the evidence upon which such findings were based, and list the names of witnesses who testified, with the exception of those whose identities have been withheld for their own protection. The Government shall, within a reasonable period of time, either reply to the report of the investigation, or indicate the steps to be taken in response to it.

Legal Proceedings

18. Governments shall ensure that persons identified by the investigation as having participated in extra-legal, arbitrary and summary executions in any

territory under their jurisdiction are brought to justice. Governments shall either bring such persons to justice or cooperate to extradite any such persons to other countries wishing to exercise jurisdiction. This principle shall apply irrespective of who and where the perpetrators or the victims are, their nationalities or where the offence was committed.

19. Without prejudice to Principle 3 above, an order from a superior officer or a public authority may not be invoked as a justification for extra-legal, arbitrary or summary executions. Superiors, officers or other public officials may be held responsible for acts committed by officials under their hierarchical authority if they had a reasonable opportunity to prevent such acts. In no circumstances including a state of war, siege or other public emergency, shall blanket immunity from prosecution be granted to any person allegedly involved in extra-legal, arbitrary or summary executions.

20. The families and dependents of victims of extra-legal, arbitrary and summary executions shall be entitled to fair and adequate compensation, within a reasonable period of time.

Principles for the Protection of Persons with Mental Illness and for the Improvement of Mental Health Care

(United Nations, 1991)

In March 1977 the UN Sub-Commission on Prevention of Discrimination and Protection of Minorities was asked to study the question of the protection of persons detained on the grounds of mental ill-health, with a view to formulating guidelines. In 1980 Mrs Erica-Irene Daes was appointed a Special Rapporteur and she submitted her final report in 1983. A working group was then established to prepare guidelines. The working group under the chairmanship of Mrs Claire Palley presented its report and draft body of principles in 1988. These draft principles were further revised by an open-ended working group and transmitted to the United Nations General Assembly. They were adopted by resolution no. 46/199 of the UN General Assembly in December 1991. The principles and their accompanying introduction are reprinted below.

Introduction

1. International interest in the treatment of persons with mental illness has increased in recent years. The United Nations has for many years been concerned with the protection of disadvantaged persons whose rights are often restricted. Persons with mental illness are especially vulnerable and require particular protection. It is essential that their rights be clearly defined and established in accordance with the International Bill of Human Rights.

2. Scientific and technological developments provide increasing opportunities for better conditions of life. However, they can give rise to social problems, as well as threaten fundamental freedoms and human rights. Similarly, medical and psychotherapeutic technology can constitute a threat to the physical and intellectual integrity of the individual.

3. There have been disturbing reports that scientific and technological products and methods have been misused, especially in the treatment of persons detained on grounds of mental illness.

4. Procedures under mental health law, including those governing access to independent and impartial bodies, are of cardinal importance to the

freedom of patients, whose human and legal rights should be protected by every means.

5. The Principles are not intended to cover every legal, medical, social and ethical aspect related to a patient's admission to an institution or his or her detention, treatment, discharge and rehabilitation in the community. In view of the great variety of legal, medical, social, economic and geographical conditions of the world community, it is obvious that not all the Principles are capable of immediate application in all countries at all times.

6. The Principles are concerned with the protection of persons with mental illness and with the improvement of mental health care. They focus in particular on the small minority of patients suffering from mental illness who need to be admitted involuntarily to a mental health facility. The large majority of people with mental illness who receive treatment are not admitted to a hospital. Of the small minority who require admission, most enter hospital on a voluntary basis. Only a few require involuntary hospitalization. Facilities for the care, support, treatment and rehabilitation of persons suffering from mental illness should, as far as possible, be provided in the community in which they live. Admission to a mental health facility should therefore take place only when such community facilities are not appropriate or not available. The provision of more resources to make alternative, less restrictive, mental health services available will help to ensure that the Principles are easier to adhere to.

7. While it is important to protect mentally ill persons from abuse and to ensure that the label of mental illness is not an excuse for inappropriately limiting the rights of people, it is equally important to protect mentally ill persons from neglect and to ensure that their needs for care and treatment, especially those of persons integrated in the community, are satisfied.

8. The Principles are intended to serve, *inter alia*, as a guide to Governments, specialized agencies, national, regional and international organizations, competent non-governmental organizations and individuals and to stimulate a constant endeavour to overcome economic and other practical difficulties in the way of their adoption and application, since they represent minimum United Nations standards for the protection of fundamental freedoms and human and legal rights of persons with mental illness.

9. Accordingly, Governments should consider adapting their laws, if necessary, to the Principles or should adopt provisions in accordance with them when introducing new relevant legislation. The Principles set the minimum United Nations standards for the protection of patients.

Principles for the Protection of Persons with Mental Illness and for the Improvement of Mental Health Care

Application

These Principles shall be applied without discrimination of any kind such as on grounds of disability, race, colour, sex, language, religion, political or other opinion, national, ethnic or social origin, legal or social status, age, property or birth.

Definitions

In these Principles:

"counsel" means a legal or other qualified representative;

"independent authority" means a competent and independent authority prescribed by domestic law;

"mental health care" includes analysis and diagnosis of a person's mental condition, and treatment, care and rehabilitation for a mental illness or suspected mental illness;

"mental health facility" means any establishment, or any unit of an establishment, which as its primary function provides mental health care;

"mental health practitioner" means a medical doctor, clinical psychologist, nurse, social worker or other appropriately trained and qualified person with specific skills relevant to mental health care;

"patient" means a person receiving mental health care and includes all persons who are admitted to a mental health facility;

"personal representative" means a person charged by law with the duty of representing a patient's interests in any specified respect or of exercising specified rights on the patient's behalf, and includes the parent or legal guardian of a minor unless otherwise provided by domestic law;

"the review body" means the body established in accordance with Principle 17 to review the involuntary admission or retention of a patient in a mental health facility.

General Limitation Clause

The exercise of the rights set forth in these Principles may be subject only to such limitations as are prescribed by law and are necessary to protect the health or safety of the person concerned or of others, or otherwise to protect public safety, order, health or morals, or the fundamental rights and freedoms of others.

Principle 1
Fundamental Freedoms and Basic Rights

1. All persons have the right to the best available mental health care, which shall be part of the health and social care system.

2. All persons with a mental illness, or who are being treated as such persons, shall be treated with humanity and respect for the inherent dignity of the human person.

3. All persons with a mental illness, or who are being treated as such persons, have the right to protection from economic, sexual and other forms of exploitation, physical or other abuse and degrading treatment.

4. There shall be no discrimination on the grounds of mental illness. "Discrimination" means any distinction, exclusion or preference that has the effect of nullifying or impairing equal enjoyment of rights. Special measures solely to protect the rights, or secure the advancement, of persons with mental illness shall not be deemed to be discriminatory. Discrimination does not include any distinction, exclusion or preference undertaken in accordance with the provisions of these Principles and necessary to protect the human rights of a person with a mental illness or of other individuals.

5. Every person with a mental illness shall have the right to exercise all civil, political, economic, social and cultural rights as recognized in the Universal Declaration of Human Rights, the International Covenant on Economic, Social and Cultural Rights, the International Covenant on Civil and Political Rights and in other relevant instruments such as the Declaration on the Rights of Disabled Persons and the Body of Principles for the Protection of All Persons under Any Form of Detention or Imprisonment.

6. Any decision that, by reason of his or her mental illness, a person lacks legal capacity, and any decision that, in consequence of such incapacity, a personal representative shall be appointed, shall be made only after a fair hearing by an independent and impartial tribunal established by domestic law. The person whose capacity is in issue shall be entitled to be represented by a counsel. If the person whose capacity is at issue does not himself or herself secure such representation it shall be made available without payment by that person to the extent that he or she does not have sufficient means to pay for it. The counsel shall not in the same proceedings represent a mental health facility or its personnel and shall not also represent a member of the family of the person whose capacity is at issue unless the tribunal is satisfied that

there is no conflict of interest. Decisions regarding capacity and the need for a personal representative shall be reviewed at reasonable intervals prescribed by domestic law. The person whose capacity is at issue, his or her personal representative, if any, and any other interested person shall have the right to appeal to a higher court against any such decision.

7. Where a court or other competent tribunal finds that a person with mental illness is unable to manage his or her own affairs, measures shall be taken, so far as is necessary and appropriate to that person's condition, to ensure the protection of his or her interests.

Principle 2
Protection of Minors

Special care should be given within the purposes of these Principles and within the context of domestic law relating to the protection of minors to protect the rights of minors, including, if necessary, the appointment of a personal representative other than a family member.

Principle 3
Life in the Community

Every person with a mental illness shall have the right to live and work, as far as possible, in the community.

Principle 4
Determination of Mental Illness

1. A determination that a person has a mental illness shall be made in accordance with internationally accepted medical standards.

2. A determination of mental illness shall never be made on the basis of political, economic or social status, or membership of a cultural, racial or religious group, or any other reason not directly relevant to mental health status.

3. Family or professional conflict, or non-conformity with moral, social, cultural or political values or religious beliefs prevailing in a person's community, shall never be a determining factor in diagnosing mental illness.

4. A background of past treatment or hospitalization as a patient shall not of itself justify any present or future determination of mental illness.

5. No person or authority shall classify a person as having, or otherwise indicate that a person has, a mental illness except for purposes directly relating to mental illness or the consequences of mental illness.

Principle 5
Medical Examination

No person shall be compelled to undergo medical examination with a view to determining whether or not he or she has a mental illness except in accordance with a procedure authorized by domestic law.

Principle 6
Confidentiality

The right of confidentiality of information concerning all persons to whom these Principles apply shall be respected.

Principle 7
Role of Community and Culture

1. Every patient shall have the right to be treated and cared for, as far as possible, in the community in which he or she lives.

2. Where treatment takes place in a mental health facility, a patient shall have the right, whenever possible, to be treated near his or her home or the home of his or her relatives or friends and shall have the right to return to the community as soon as possible.

3. Every patient shall have the right to treatment suited to his or her cultural background.

Principle 8
Standards of Care

1. Every patient shall have the right to receive such health and social care as is appropriate to his or her health needs, and is entitled to care and treatment in accordance with the same standards as other ill persons.

2. Every patient shall be protected from harm, including unjustified medication, abuse by other patients, staff or others or other acts causing mental distress or physical discomfort.

Principle 9
Treatment

1. Every patient shall have the right to be treated in the least restrictive environment and with the least restrictive or intrusive treatment appropriate to the patient's health needs and the need to protect the physical safety of others.

2. The treatment and care of every patient shall be based on an individually prescribed plan, discussed with the patient, reviewed regularly, revised as necessary and provided by qualified professional staff.

3. Mental health care shall always be provided in accordance with applicable standards of ethics for mental health practitioners, including internationally accepted standards such as the Principles of Medical Ethics adopted by the United Nations General Assembly. Mental health knowledge and skills shall never be abused.

4. The treatment of every patient shall be directed towards preserving and enhancing personal autonomy.

Principle 10
Medication

1. Medication shall meet the best health needs of the patient, shall be given to a patient only for therapeutic or diagnostic purposes and shall never be administered as a punishment, or for the convenience of others. Subject to the provisions of paragraph 15 of Principle 11, mental health practitioners shall only administer medication of known or demonstrated efficacy.

2. All medication shall be prescribed by a mental health practitioner authorized by law and shall be recorded in the patient's records.

Principle 11
Consent to Treatment

1. No treatment shall be given to a patient without his or her informed consent, except as provided for in paragraphs 6, 7, 8, 13 and 15 below.

2. Informed consent is consent obtained freely without threats or improper inducements after appropriate disclosure to the patient of adequate and understandable information in a form and language understood by the patient on:

a) The diagnostic assessment;

b) The purpose, method, likely duration and expected benefit of the proposed treatment;

c) Alternative modes of treatment, including those less intrusive; and

d) Possible pain or discomfort, risks and side-effects of the proposed treatment.

3. A patient may request the presence of a person or persons of the patient's choosing during the procedure for granting consent.

4. A patient has the right to refuse or stop treatment except as provided for in paragraphs 6, 7, 8, 13 and 15 below. The consequences of refusing or stopping treatment must be explained to the patient.

5. A patient shall never be invited or induced to waive the right to informed consent. If the patient should seek to do so, it shall be explained to the patient that the treatment cannot be given without informed consent.

6. Except as provided in paragraphs 7, 8, 12, 13, 14 and 15 below, a proposed plan of treatment may be given to a patient without a patient's informed consent if the following conditions are satisfied:

a) The patient is, at the relevant time, held as an involuntary patient;

b) An independent authority, having in its possession all relevant information, including the information specified in paragraph 2 above, is satisfied that, at the relevant time, the patient lacks the capacity to give or withhold informed consent to the proposed plan of treatment or, if domestic legislation so provides, that, having regard to the patient's own safety or the safety of others, the patient unreasonably withholds such consent; and

c) The independent authority is satisfied that the proposed plan of treatment is in the best interests of the patient's health needs.

7. Paragraph 6 above does not apply to a patient with a personal representative empowered by law to consent to treatment for the patient; but, except as provided in paragraphs 12, 13, 14 and 15 below, treatment may be given to such a patient without his or her informed consent if the personal representative, having been given the information described in paragraph 2 above, consents on the patient's behalf.

8. Except as provided in paragraphs 12, 13, 14 and 15 below, treatment may also be given to any patient without the patient's informed consent if a qualified mental health practitioner authorized by law determines that it is urgently necessary in order to prevent immediate or imminent harm to the patient or to other persons. Such treatment shall not be prolonged beyond the period that is strictly necessary for this purpose.

9. Where any treatment is authorized without the patient's informed consent, every effort shall nevertheless be made to inform the patient about the nature of the treatment and any possible alternatives and to involve the patient as far as practicable in the development of the treatment plan.

10. All treatment shall be immediately recorded in the patient's medical records, with an indication of whether involuntary or voluntary.

11. Physical restraint or involuntary seclusion of a patient shall not be employed except in accordance with the officially approved procedures of the mental health facility and only when it is the only means available to prevent immediate or imminent harm to the patient or others. It shall not be prolonged beyond the period which is strictly necessary for this purpose. All instances of physical restraint or involuntary seclusion, the reasons for them, and their nature and extent shall be recorded in the patient's medical record. A patient who is restrained or secluded shall be kept under humane conditions

and be under the care and close and regular supervision of qualified members of the staff. A personal representative, if any and if relevant, shall be given prompt notice of any physical restraint or involuntary seclusion of the patient.

12. Sterilization shall never be carried out as a treatment for mental illness.

13. A major medical or surgical procedure may be carried out on a person with mental illness only where it is permitted by domestic law, where it is considered that it would best serve the health needs of the patient and where the patient gives informed consent, except that, where the patient is unable to give informed consent, the procedure shall be authorized only after independent review.

14. Psychosurgery and other intrusive and irreversible treatments for mental illness shall never be carried out on a patient who is an involuntary patient in a mental health facility; and, to the extent that domestic law permits them to be carried out, they may be carried out on any other patient only where the patient has given informed consent and an independent external body has satisfied itself that there is genuine informed consent and that the treatment best serves the health needs of the patient.

15. Clinical trials and experimental treatment shall never be carried out on any patient without informed consent, except that a patient who is unable to give informed consent may be admitted to a clinical trial or given experimental treatment but only with the approval of a competent, independent review body specifically constituted for this purpose.

16. In the cases specified in paragraphs 6, 7, 8, 13, 14 and 15 above, the patient or his or her personal representative, or any interested person, shall have the right to appeal to a judicial or other independent authority concerning any treatment given to him or her.

Principle 12
Notice of Rights

1. A patient in a mental health facility shall be informed as soon as possible after admission, in a form and a language which the patient understands, of all his or her rights in accordance with these Principles and under domestic law, which information shall include an explanation of those rights and how to exercise them.

2. If and for so long as a patient is unable to understand such information, the rights of the patient shall be communicated to the personal representative, if any and if appropriate, and to the person or persons best able to represent the patient's interests and willing to do so.

3. A patient who has the necessary capacity has the right to nominate a person who should be informed on his or her behalf as well as a person to represent his or her interests to the authorities of the facility.

Principle 13
Rights and Conditions in Mental Health Facilities

1. Every patient in a mental health facility shall, in particular, have the right to full respect for his or her:

a) Recognition everywhere as a person before the law;

b) Privacy;

c) Freedom of communication which includes freedom to communicate with other persons in the facility; freedom to send and receive uncensored private communications; freedom to receive, in private, visits from a counsel or personal representative and, at all reasonable times, from other visitors; and freedom of access to postal and telephone services and to newspapers, radio and television;

d) Freedom of religion or belief.

2. The environment and living conditions in mental health facilities shall be as close as possible to those of the normal life of persons of similar age and in particular shall include:

a) Facilities for recreational and leisure activities;

b) Facilities for education;

c) Facilities to purchase or receive items for daily living, recreation and communication;

d) Facilities, and encouragement to use such facilities, for a patient's engagement in an active occupation suited to his or her social and cultural background, and for appropriate vocational rehabilitation measures to promote reintegration in the community. These measures should include vocational guidance, vocational training and placement services to enable patients to secure or retain employment in the community.

3. In no circumstances shall a patient be subject to forced labour. Within the limits compatible with the needs of the patient and with the requirements of institutional administration, a patient shall be able to choose the type of work he or she wishes to perform.

4. The labour of a patient in a mental health facility shall not be exploited. Every such patient shall have the right to receive the same remuneration for any work which he or she does as would, according to domestic law or custom, be paid for such work to a non-patient. Every such patient shall in any event have the right to receive a fair share of any remuneration which is paid to the mental health facility for his or her work.

Principle 14
Resources for Mental Health Facilities

1. A mental health facility shall have access to the same level of resources as any other health establishment, and in particular:

a) Qualified medical and other appropriate professional staff in sufficient numbers and with adequate space to provide each patient with privacy and a programme of appropriate and active therapy;

b) Diagnostic and therapeutic equipment for the patient;

c) Appropriate professional care; and

d) Adequate, regular and comprehensive treatment, including supplies of medication.

2. Every mental health facility shall be inspected by the competent authorities with sufficient frequency to ensure that the conditions, treatment, and care of patients comply with these Principles.

Principle 15
Admission Principles

1. Where a person needs treatment in a mental health facility, every effort shall be made to avoid involuntary admission.

2. Access to a mental health facility shall be administered in the same way as access to any other facility for any other illness.

3. Every patient not admitted involuntarily shall have the right to leave the mental health facility at any time unless the criteria for his or her retention as an involuntary patient, as set forth in Principle 16, apply, and he or she shall be informed of that right.

Principle 16
Involuntary Admission

1. A person may (a) be admitted involuntarily to a mental health facility as a patient; or (b) having already been admitted voluntarily as a patient, be retained as an involuntary patient in the mental health facility if, and only if, a qualified mental health practitioner authorized by law for that purpose determines, in accordance with Principle 4, that that person has a mental illness and considers:

(a) That, because of that mental illness, there is a serious likelihood of immediate or imminent harm to that person or to other persons; or

(b) That, in the case of a person whose mental illness is severe and whose judgement is impaired, failure to admit or retain that person is likely to lead to a serious deterioration in his or her condition or will prevent the giving of appropriate treatment that can only be given by admission to a mental health facility in accordance with the principle of the least restrictive alternative.

In the case referred to in subparagraph (b), a second such mental health practitioner, independent of the first, should be consulted where possible. If such consultation takes place, the involuntary admission or retention may not take place unless the second mental health practitioner concurs.

2. Involuntary admission or retention shall initially be for a short period as specified by domestic law for observation and preliminary treatment pending review of the admission or retention by the review body. The grounds of the admission shall be communicated to the patient without delay and the fact of the admission and the grounds for it shall also be communicated promptly and in detail to the review body, to the patient's personal representative, if any, and, unless the patient objects, to the patient's family.

3. A mental health facility may receive involuntarily admitted patients only if the facility has been designated to do so by a competent authority prescribed by domestic law.

Principle 17
Review Body

1. The review body shall be a judicial or other independent and impartial body established by domestic law and functioning in accordance with procedures laid down by domestic law. It shall, in formulating its decisions, have the assistance of one or more qualified and independent mental health practitioners and take their advice into account.

2. The review body's initial review, as required by paragraph 2 of Principle 16, of a decision to admit or retain a person as an involuntary patient shall take place as soon as possible after that decision and shall be conducted in accordance with simple and expeditious procedures as specified by domestic law.

3. The review body shall periodically review the cases of involuntary patients at reasonable intervals as specified by domestic law.

4. An involuntary patient may apply to the review body for release or voluntary status, at reasonable intervals as specified by domestic law.

5. At each review the review body shall consider whether the criteria for involuntary admission set out in paragraph 1 of Principle 16 are still satisfied, and, if not, the patient shall be discharged as an involuntary patient.

6. If at any time the mental health practitioner responsible for the case is satisfied that the conditions for the retention of a person as an involuntary

patient are no longer satisfied, he or she shall order the discharge of that person as such a patient.

7. A patient or his personal representative or any interested person shall have the right to appeal to a higher court against a decision that the patient be admitted to, or be retained in, a mental health facility.

Principle 18
Procedural Safeguards

1. The patient shall be entitled to choose and appoint a counsel to represent the patient as such, including representation in any complaint procedure or appeal. If the patient does not secure such services, a counsel shall be made available without payment by the patient to the extent that the patient lacks sufficient means to pay.

2. The patient shall also be entitled to the assistance, if necessary, of the services of an interpreter. Where such services are necessary and the patient does not secure them, they shall be made available without payment by the patient to the extent that the patient lacks sufficient means to pay.

3. The patient and the patient's counsel may request and produce at any hearing an independent mental health report and any other reports and oral, written and other evidence that are relevant and admissible.

4. Copies of the patient's records and any reports and documents to be submitted shall be given to the patient and to the patient's counsel except in special cases where it is determined that a specific disclosure to the patient would cause serious harm to the patient's health or put at risk the safety of others. As domestic law may provide, any document not given to the patient should, when this can be done in confidence, be given to the patient's personal representative and counsel. When any part of a document is withheld from a patient, the patient or the patient's counsel, if any, shall receive notice of the withholding and the reasons for it and it shall be subject to judicial review.

5. The patient and the patient's personal representative and counsel shall be entitled to attend, participate and be heard personally in any hearing.

6. If the patient or the patient's personal representative or counsel requests that a particular person be present at a hearing, that person shall be admitted unless it is determined that the person's presence could cause serious harm to the patient's health or put at risk the safety of others.

7. Any decision whether the hearing or any part of it shall be in public or in private and may be publicly reported shall give full consideration to the patient's own wishes, to the need to respect the privacy of the patient and of

other persons and to the need to prevent serious harm to the patient's health or to avoid putting at risk the safety of others.

8. The decision arising out of the hearing and the reasons for it shall be expressed in writing. Copies shall be given to the patient and his or her personal representative and counsel. In deciding whether the decision shall be published in whole or in part, full consideration shall be given to the patient's own wishes, to the need to respect his or her privacy and that of other persons, to the public interest in the open administration of justice and to the need to prevent serious harm to the patient's health or to avoid putting at risk the safety of others.

Principle 19
Access to Information

1. A patient (which term in this Principle includes a former patient) shall be entitled to have access to the information concerning the patient in his or her health and personal records maintained by a mental health facility. This right may be subject to restrictions in order to prevent serious harm to the patient's health and avoid putting at risk the safety of others. As domestic law may provide, any such information not given to the patient should, when this can be done in confidence, be given to the patient's personal representative and counsel. When any of the information is withheld from a patient, the patient or the patient's counsel, if any, shall receive notice of the withholding and the reasons for it and it shall be subject to judicial review.

2. Any written comments by the patient or the patient's personal representative or counsel shall, on request, be inserted in the patient's file.

Principle 20
Criminal Offenders

1. This Principle applies to persons serving sentences of imprisonment for criminal offences, or who are otherwise detained in the course of criminal proceedings or investigations against them, and who are determined to have a mental illness or who it is believed may have such an illness.

2. All such persons should receive the best available mental health care as provided in Principle 1. These Principles shall apply to them to the fullest extent possible, with only such limited modifications and exceptions as are necessary in the circumstances. No such modifications and exceptions shall prejudice the persons' rights under the instruments noted in paragraph 5 of Principle 1.

3. Domestic law may authorize a court or other competent authority, acting on the basis of competent and independent medical advice, to order that such persons be admitted to a mental health facility.

4. Treatment of persons determined to have a mental illness shall in all circumstances be consistent with Principle 11.

Principle 21
Complaints

Every patient and former patient shall have the right to make a complaint through procedures as specified by domestic law.

Principle 22
Monitoring and Remedies

States shall ensure that appropriate mechanisms are in force to promote compliance with these Principles, for the inspection of mental health facilities, for the submission, investigation and resolution of complaints and for the institution of appropriate disciplinary or judicial proceedings for professional misconduct or violation of the rights of a patient.

Principle 23
Implementation

1. States should implement these Principles through appropriate legislative, judicial, administrative, educational and other measures which they shall review periodically.

2. States shall make these Principles widely known by appropriate and active means.

Principle 24
Scope of Principles Relating to Mental Health Facilities

These Principles apply to all persons who are admitted to a mental health facility.

Principle 25
Saving of Existing Rights

There shall be no restriction upon or derogation from any existing rights of patients, including rights recognized in applicable international or domestic law, on the pretext that these Principles do not recognize such rights or that they recognize them to a lesser extent.

Body of Principles for the Protection of All Persons Under Any Form of Detention or Imprisonment
(United Nations, 1988)

In the mid-1970s, the United Nations recognized the need to compile in one instrument a wide-ranging set of detailed practical safeguards aimed at protecting all detainees from abuses such as arbitrary detention, coercive interrogation, torture or other ill-treatment and "disappearance". After more than a decade of drafting the UN General Assembly on 9 December 1988 adopted by consensus the UN Body of Principles for the Protection of All Persons under Any Form of Detention or Imprisonment. These principles stress the importance of detainees having access to the outside world and of independent supervision of detention conditions. The preamble to the principles has been omitted here.

Body of Principles for the Protection of All Persons Under Any Form of Detention or Imprisonment

Scope of the Body of Principles

These principles apply for the protection of all persons under any form of detention or imprisonment.

Use of Terms

For the purposes of the Body of Principles:

(a) "Arrest" means the act of apprehending a person for the alleged commission of an offence or by the action of an authority;

(b) "Detained" person means any person deprived of personal liberty except as a result of conviction for an offence;

(c) "Imprisoned person" means any person deprived of personal liberty as a result of conviction for an offence;

(d) "Detention" means the condition of detained persons as defined above;

(e) "Imprisonment" means the condition of imprisoned persons as defined above;

(f) The words "a judicial or other authority" mean a judicial or other authority under the law whose status and tenure should afford the strongest possible guarantees of competence, impartiality and independence.

Principle 1

All persons under any form of detention or imprisonment shall be treated in a humane manner and with respect for the inherent dignity of the human person.

Principle 2

Arrest, detention or imprisonment shall only be carried out strictly in accordance with the provisions of the law and by competent officials or persons authorized for that purpose.

Principle 3

There shall be no restriction upon or derogation from any of the human rights of persons under any form of detention or imprisonment recognized or existing in any State pursuant to law, conventions, regulations or custom on the pretext that this Body of Principles does not recognize such rights or that it recognizes them to a lesser extent.

Principle 4

Any form of detention or imprisonment and all measures affecting the human rights of a person under any form of detention or imprisonment shall be ordered by, or be subject to the effective control of, a judicial or other authority.

Principle 5

1. These principles shall be applied to all persons within the territory of any given State, without distinction of any kind, such as race, colour, sex, language, religion or religious belief, political or other opinion, national, ethnic or social origin, property, birth or other status.

2. Measures applied under the law and designed solely to protect the rights and special status of women, especially pregnant women and nursing mothers, children and juveniles, aged, sick or handicapped persons shall not be deemed to be discriminatory. The need for, and the application of, such measures shall always be subject to review by a judicial or other authority.

Principle 6

No person under any form of detention or imprisonment shall be subjected to torture or to cruel, inhuman or degrading treatment or punishment.[1] No circumstance whatever may be invoked as a justification for torture or other cruel, inhuman or degrading treatment or punishment.

Principle 7

1. States should prohibit by law any act contrary to the rights and duties contained in these principles, make any such act subject to appropriate sanctions and conduct impartial investigations upon complaints.

2. Officials who have reason to believe that a violation of this Body of Principles has occurred or is about to occur shall report the matter to their superior authorities and, where necessary, to other appropriate authorities or organs vested with reviewing or remedial powers.

3. Any other person who has ground to believe that a violation of this Body of Principles has occurred or is about to occur shall have the right to report the matter to the superiors of the officials involved as well as to other appropriate authorities or organs vested with reviewing or remedial powers.

Principle 8

Persons in detention shall be subject to treatment appropriate to their unconvicted status. Accordingly, they shall, whenever possible, be kept separate from imprisoned persons.

Principle 9

The authorities which arrest a person, keep him under detention or investigate the case shall exercise only the powers granted to them under the law and the exercise of these powers shall be subject to recourse to a judicial or other authority.

Principle 10

Anyone who is arrested shall be informed at the time of his arrest of the reason for his arrest and shall be promptly informed of any charges against him.

---

[1]The term "cruel, inhuman or degrading treatment or punishment" should be interpreted so as to extend the widest possible protection against abuses, whether physical or mental, including the holding of a detained or imprisoned person in conditions which deprive him, temporarily or permanently, of the use of any of his natural senses, such as sight or hearing, or of his awareness of place and the passing of time.

Principle 11

1. A person shall not be kept in detention without being given an effective opportunity to be heard promptly by a judicial or other authority. A detained person shall have the right to defend himself or to be assisted by counsel as prescribed by law.

2. A detained person and his counsel, if any, shall receive prompt and full communication of any order of detention, together with the reasons therefor.

3. A judicial or other authority shall be empowered to review as appropriate the continuance of detention.

Principle 12

1. There shall be duly recorded:

(a)   The reasons for the arrest;

(b)   The time of the arrest and the taking of the arrested person to a place of custody as well as that of his first appearance before a judicial or other authority;

(c)   The identity of the law enforcement officials concerned;

(d)   Precise information concerning the place of custody.

2. Such records shall be communicated to the detained person, or his counsel, if any, in the form prescribed by law.

Principle 13

Any person shall, at the moment of arrest and at the commencement of detention or imprisonment, or promptly thereafter, be provided by the authority responsible for his arrest, detention or imprisonment, respectively, with information on and an explanation of his rights and how to avail himself of such rights.

Principle 14

A person who does not adequately understand or speak the language used by the authorities responsible for his arrest, detention or imprisonment is entitled to receive promptly in a language which he understands the information referred to in principle 10, principle 11, paragraph 2, principle 12, paragraph 1, and principle 13 and to have the assistance, free of charge, if necessary, of an interpreter in connection with legal proceedings subsequent to his arrest.

Principle 15

Notwithstanding the exceptions contained in principle 16, paragraph 4, and principle 18, paragraph 3, communication of the detained or imprisoned person with the outside world, and in particular his family or counsel, shall not be denied for more than a matter of days.

Principle 16

1. Promptly after arrest and after each transfer from one place of detention or imprisonment to another, a detained or imprisoned person shall be entitled to notify or to require the competent authority to notify members of his family or other appropriate persons of his choice of his arrest, detention or imprisonment or of the transfer and of the place where he is kept in custody.

2. If a detained or imprisoned person is a foreigner, he shall also be promptly informed of his right to communicate by appropriate means with a consular post or the diplomatic mission of the State of which he is a national or which is otherwise entitled to receive such communication in accordance with international law or with the representative of the competent international organization, if he is a refugee or is otherwise under the protection of an intergovernmental organization.

3. If a detained or imprisoned person is a juvenile or is incapable of understanding his entitlement, the competent authority shall on its own initiative undertake the notification referred to in the present principle. Special attention shall be given to notifying parents or guardians.

4. Any notification referred to in the present principle shall be made or permitted to be made without delay. The competent authority may however delay a notification for a reasonable period where exceptional needs of the investigation so require.

Principle 17

1. A detained person shall be entitled to have the assistance of a legal counsel. He shall be informed of his right by the competent authority promptly after arrest and shall be provided with reasonable facilities for exercising it.

2. If a detained person does not have a legal counsel of his own choice, he shall be entitled to have a legal counsel assigned to him by a judicial or other authority in all cases where the interests of justice so require and without payment by him if he does not have sufficient means to pay.

Principle 18

1. A detained or imprisoned person shall be entitled to communicate and consult with his legal counsel.

2. A detained or imprisoned person shall be allowed adequate time and facilities for consultations with his legal counsel.

3. The right of a detained or imprisoned person to be visited by and to consult and communicate, without delay or censorship and in full confidentiality, with his legal counsel may not be suspended or restricted save

in exceptional circumstances, to be specified by law or lawful regulations, when it is considered indispensable by a judicial or other authority in order to maintain security and good order.

4. Interviews between a detained or imprisoned person and his legal counsel may be within sight, but not within the hearing, of a law enforcement official.

5. Communications between a detained or imprisoned person and his legal counsel mentioned in the present principle shall be inadmissible as evidence against the detained or imprisoned person unless they are connected with a continuing or contemplated crime.

Principle 19

A detained or imprisoned person shall have the right to be visited by and to correspond with, in particular, members of his family and shall be given adequate opportunity to communicate with the outside world, subject to reasonable conditions and restrictions as specified by law or lawful regulations.

Principle 20

If a detained or imprisoned person so requests, he shall if possible be kept in a place of detention or imprisonment reasonably near his usual place of residence.

Principle 21

1. It shall be prohibited to take undue advantage of the situation of a detained or imprisoned person for the purpose of compelling him to confess, to incriminate himself otherwise or to testify against any other person.

2. No detained person while being interrogated shall be subject to violence, threats or methods of interrogation which impair his capacity of decision or his judgement.

Principle 22

No detained or imprisoned person shall, even with his consent, be subjected to any medical or scientific experimentation which may be detrimental to his health.

Principle 23

1. The duration of any interrogation of a detained or imprisoned person and of the intervals between interrogations as well as the identity of the officials who conducted the interrogations and other persons present shall be recorded and certified in such form as may be prescribed by law.

2. A detained or imprisoned person, or his counsel when provided by law, shall have access to the information described in paragraph 1 of the present principle.

Principle 24

A proper medical examination shall be offered to a detained or imprisoned person as promptly as possible after his admission to the place of detention or imprisonment, and thereafter medical care and treatment shall be provided whenever necessary. This care and treatment shall be provided free of charge.

Principle 25

A detained or imprisoned person or his counsel shall, subject only to reasonable conditions to ensure security and good order in the place of detention or imprisonment, have the right to request or petition a judicial or other authority for a second medical examination or opinion.

Principle 26

The fact that a detained or imprisoned person underwent a medical examination, the name of the physician and the results of such an examination shall be duly recorded. Access to such records shall be ensured. Modalities therefor shall be in accordance with relevant rules of domestic law.

Principle 27

Non-compliance with these Principles in obtaining evidence shall be taken into account in determining the admissibility of such evidence against a detained or imprisoned person.

Principle 28

A detained or imprisoned person shall have the right to obtain within the limits of available resources, if from public sources, reasonable quantities of educational, cultural and informational material, subject to reasonable conditions to ensure security and good order in the place of detention or imprisonment.

Principle 29

1. In order to supervise the strict observance of relevant laws and regulations, places of detention shall be visited regularly by qualified and experienced persons appointed by, and responsible to, a competent authority distinct from the authority directly in charge of the administration of the place of detention or imprisonment.

2. A detained or imprisoned person shall have the right to communicate freely and in full confidentiality with the persons who visit the places of

detention or imprisonment in accordance with paragraph 1 of the present principle, subject to reasonable conditions to ensure security and good order in such places.

Principle 30

1. The types of conduct of the detained or imprisoned person that constitute disciplinary offences during detention or imprisonment, the description and duration of disciplinary punishment that may be inflicted and the authorities competent to impose such punishment shall be specified by law or lawful regulations and duly published.

2. A detained or imprisoned person shall have the right to be heard before disciplinary action is taken. He shall have the right to bring such action to higher authorities for review.

Principle 31

The appropriate authorities shall endeavour to ensure, according to domestic law, assistance when needed to dependent and, in particular, minor members of the families of detained or imprisoned persons and shall devote a particular measure of care to the appropriate custody of children left without supervision.

Principle 32

1. A detained person or his counsel shall be entitled at any time to take proceedings according to domestic law before a judicial or other authority to challenge the lawfulness of his detention in order to obtain his release without delay, if it is unlawful.

2. The proceedings referred to in paragraph 1 of the present principle shall be simple and expeditious and at no cost for detained persons without adequate means. The detaining authority shall produce without unreasonable delay the detained person before the reviewing authority.

Principle 33

1. A detained or imprisoned person or his counsel shall have the right to make a request or complaint regarding his treatment, in particular in case of torture or other cruel, inhuman or degrading treatment, to the authorities responsible for the administration of the place of detention and to higher authorities and, when necessary, to appropriate authorities vested with reviewing or remedial powers.

2. In those cases where neither the detained or imprisoned person nor his counsel has the possibility to exercise his rights under paragraph 1 of the present principle, a member of the family of the detained or imprisoned

person or any other person who has knowledge of the case may exercise such rights.

3. Confidentiality concerning the request or complaint shall be maintained if so requested by the complainant.

4. Every request or complaint shall be promptly dealt with and replied to without undue delay. If the request or complaint is rejected or, in case of inordinate delay, the complainant shall be entitled to bring it before a judicial or other authority. Neither the detained or imprisoned person nor any complainant under paragraph 1 of the present principle shall suffer prejudice for making a request or complaint.

Principle 34

Whenever the death or disappearance of a detained or imprisoned person occurs during his detention or imprisonment, an inquiry into the cause of death or disappearance shall be held by a judicial or other authority, either on its own motion or at the instance of a member of the family of such a person or any person who has knowledge of the case. When circumstances so warrant, such an inquiry shall be held on the same procedural basis whenever the death or disappearance occurs shortly after the termination of the detention or imprisonment. The findings of such inquiry or a report thereon shall be made available upon request, unless doing so would jeopardize an ongoing criminal investigation.

Principle 35

1. Damage incurred because of acts or omissions by a public official contrary to the rights contained in these Principles shall be compensated according to the applicable rules on liability provided by domestic law.

2. Information required to be recorded under these Principles shall be available in accordance with procedures provided by domestic law for use in claiming compensation under the present principle.

Principle 36

1. A detained person suspected of or charged with a criminal offence shall be presumed innocent and shall be treated as such until proved guilty according to law in a public trial at which he has had all the guarantees necessary for his defence.

2. The arrest or detention of such a person pending investigation and trial shall be carried out only for the purposes of the administration of justice on grounds and under conditions and procedures specified by law. The imposition of restrictions upon such a person which are not strictly required for the purpose of the detention or to prevent hindrance to the process of

investigation or the administration of justice, or for the maintenance of security and good order in the place of detention shall be forbidden.

Principle 37

A person detained on a criminal charge shall be brought before a judicial or other authority provided by law promptly after his arrest. Such authority shall decide without delay upon the lawfulness and necessity of detention. No person may be kept under detention pending investigation or trial except upon the written order of such an authority. A detained person shall, when brought before such an authority, have the right to make a statement on the treatment received by him while in custody.

Principle 38

A person detained on a criminal charge shall be entitled to trial within a reasonable time or to release pending trial.

Principle 39

Except in special cases provided for by law, a person detained on a criminal charge shall be entitled, unless a judicial or other authority decides otherwise in the interest of the administration of justice, to release pending trial subject to the conditions that may be imposed in accordance with the law. Such authority shall keep the necessity of detention under review.

General clause

Nothing in this Body of Principles shall be construed as restricting or derogating from any right defined in the International Covenant on Civil and Political Rights.

Standard Minimum Rules for the Treatment of Prisoners and Procedures for the Effective Implementation of the Standard Minimum Rules

(United Nations, 1955, 1977, 1984)

These rules were adopted by the first United Nations Congress on the Prevention of Crime and the Treatment of Offenders, held at Geneva in 1955. Rule 95 was added in 1977.

The rules have been edited to exclude Rules 46-47 and 50-51 (Institutional personnel); Rules 63-64 (Individualization of regime); Rules 67-69 (Classification and individualization); Rule 70 (Privileges); Rules 73-76 (Work); Rule 81 (Social Relations and after-care).

The Procedures for the Effective Implementation of the Standard Minimum Rules were approved by the United Nations' Economic and Social Council at its 21st Plenary Session in May 1984. The Procedures are reprinted here in an abridged form. The full document is published by the United Nations' Department of Public Information, (DPI/832, New York, 1984).

Standard Minimum Rules for the Treatment of Prisoners

Preliminary Observations

1. The following rules are not intended to describe in detail a model system of penal institutions. They seek only, on the basis of the general consensus of contemporary thought and the essential elements of the most adequate systems of today, to set out what is generally accepted as being good principle and practice in the treatment of prisoners and the management of institutions.

2. In view of the great variety of legal, social, economic and geographical conditions of the world, it is evident that not all of the rules are capable of application in all places and at all times. They should, however, serve to stimulate a constant endeavour to overcome practical difficulties in the way of their application, in the knowledge that they represent, as a whole, the minimum conditions which are accepted as suitable by the United Nations.

3. On the other hand, the rules cover a field in which thought is constantly developing. They are not intended to preclude experiment and practices,

provided these are in harmony with the principles and seek to further the purposes which derive from the text of the rules as a whole. It will always be justifiable for the central prison administration to authorize departures from the rules in this spirit.

4. (1) Part I of the rules covers the general management of institutions, and is applicable to all categories of prisoners, criminal or civil, untried or convicted, including prisoners subject to "security measures" or corrective measures ordered by the judge.

(2) Part II contains rules applicable only to the special categories dealt with in each section. Nevertheless, the rules under section A, applicable to prisoners under sentence, shall be equally applicable to categories of prisoners dealt with in sections B, C and D, provided they do not conflict with the rules governing those categories and are for their benefit.

5. (1) The rules do not seek to regulate the management of institutions set aside for young persons such as Borstal institutions or correctional schools, but in general Part I would be equally applicable to such institutions.

(2) The category of young prisoners should include at least all young persons who come within the jurisdiction of juvenile courts. As a rule, such young persons should not be sentenced to imprisonment.

Part I. Rules of General Application

Basic Principle

6. (1) The following rules shall be applied impartially. There shall be no discrimination on grounds of race, colour, sex, language, religion, political or other opinion, national or social origin, property, birth or other status.

(2) On the other hand, it is necessary to respect the religious beliefs and moral precepts of the group to which a prisoner belongs.

Register

7. (1) In every place where persons are imprisoned there shall be kept a bound registration book with numbered pages in which shall be entered in respect of each prisoner received:

a) Information concerning his identity;

b) The reason for his commitment and the authority therefor;

c) The day and hour of his admission and release.

(2) No person shall be received in an institution without a valid commitment order of which the details shall have been previously entered in the register.

Separation of categories

8. The different categories of prisoners shall be kept in separate institutions or parts of institutions taking account of their sex, age, criminal record, the legal reason for their detention and the necessities of their treatment. Thus,

a) Men and women shall so far as possible be detained in separate institutions; in an institution which receives both men and women the whole of the premises allocated to women shall be entirely separate;

b) Untried prisoners shall be kept separate from convicted prisoners;

c) Persons imprisoned for debt and other civil prisoners shall be kept separate from persons imprisoned by reason of a criminal offence;

d) Young prisoners shall be kept separate from adults.

Accommodation

9. (1) Where sleeping accommodation is in individual cells or rooms, each prisoner shall occupy by night a cell or room by himself. If for special reasons, such as temporary overcrowding, it becomes necessary for the central prison administration to make an exception to this rule, it is not desirable to have two prisoners in a cell or room.

(2) Where dormitories are used, they shall be occupied by prisoners carefully selected as being suitable to associate with one another in those conditions. There shall be regular supervision by night, in keeping with the nature of the institution.

10. All accommodation provided for the use of prisoners and in particular all sleeping accommodation shall meet all requirements of health, due regard being paid to climatic conditions and particularly to cubic content of air, minimum floor space, lighting, heating and ventilation.

11. In all places where prisoners are required to live or work,

a) The windows shall be large enough to enable the prisoners to read or work, by natural light, and shall be so constructed that they can allow the entrance of fresh air whether or not there is artificial ventilation;

b) Artificial light shall be provided sufficient for the prisoners to read or work without injury to eyesight.

12. The sanitary installations shall be adequate to enable every prisoner to comply with the needs of nature when necessary and in a clean and decent manner.

13. Adequate bathing and shower installations shall be provided so that every prisoner may be enabled and required to have a bath or shower, at a temperature suitable to the climate, as frequently as necessary for general

hygiene according to season and geographical region, but at least once a week in a temperate climate.

14. All parts of an institution regularly used by prisoners shall be properly maintained and kept scrupulously clean at all times.

Personal hygiene

15. Prisoners shall be required to keep their persons clean, and to this end they shall be provided with water and with such toilet articles as are necessary for health and cleanliness.

16. In order that prisoners may maintain a good appearance compatible with their self-respect, facilities shall be provided for the proper care of the hair and beard, and men shall be enabled to shave regularly.

Clothing and bedding

17. (1) Every prisoner who is not allowed to wear his own clothing shall be provided with an outfit of clothing suitable for the climate and adequate to keep him in good health. Such clothing shall in no manner be degrading or humiliating.

(2) All clothing shall be clean and kept in proper condition. Underclothing shall be changed and washed as often as necessary for the maintenance of hygiene.

(3) In exceptional circumstances, whenever a prisoner is removed outside the institution for an authorized purpose, he shall be allowed to wear his own clothing or other inconspicuous clothing.

18. If prisoners are allowed to wear their own clothing, arrangements shall be made on their admission to the institution to ensure that it shall be clean and fit for use.

19. Every prisoner shall, in accordance with local or national standards, be provided with a separate bed, and with separate and sufficient bedding which shall be clean when issued, kept in good order and changed often enough to ensure its cleanliness.

Food

20. (1) Every prisoner shall be provided by the administration at the usual hours with food of nutritional value adequate for health and strength, of wholesome quality and well prepared and served.

(2) Drinking water shall be available to every prisoner whenever he needs it.

Exercise and sport

21. (1) Every prisoner who is not employed in outdoor work shall have at least one hour of suitable exercise in the open air daily if the weather permits.

(2) Young prisoners, and others of suitable age and physique, shall receive physical and recreational training during the period of exercise. To this end space, installations and equipment should be provided.

Medical services

22. (1) At every institution there shall be available the services of at least one qualified medical officer who should have some knowledge of psychiatry. The medical services should be organized in close relationship to the general health administration of the community or nation. They shall include a psychiatric service for the diagnosis and, in proper cases, the treatment of states of mental abnormality.

(2) Sick prisoners who require specialist treatment shall be transferred to specialized institutions or to civil hospitals. Where hospital facilities are provided in an institution, their equipment, furnishings and pharmaceutical supplies shall be proper for the medical care and treatment of sick prisoners, and there shall be a staff of suitable trained officers.

(3) The services of a qualified dental officer shall be available to every prisoner.

23. (1) In women's institutions there shall be special accommodation for all necessary pre-natal and post-natal care and treatment. Arrangements shall be made wherever practicable for children to be born in a hospital outside the institution. If a child in born in prison, this fact shall not be mentioned in the birth certificate.

(2) Where nursing infants are allowed to remain in the institution with their mothers, provision shall be made for a nursery staffed by qualified persons, where the infants shall be placed when they are not in the care of their mothers.

24. The medical officer shall see and examine every prisoner as soon as possible after his admission and thereafter as necessary, with a view particularly to the discovery of physical or mental illness and the taking of all necessary measures; the segregation of prisoners suspected of infectious or contagious conditions; the noting of physical or mental defects which might hamper rehabilitation, and the determination of the physical capacity of every prisoner for work.

25. (1) The medical officer shall have the care of the physical and mental health of the prisoners and should daily see all sick prisoners, all who

complain of illness, and any prisoner to whom his attention is specially directed.

(2) The medical officer shall report to the director whenever he considers that a prisoner's physical or mental health has been or will be injuriously affected by continued imprisonment or by any condition of imprisonment.

26. (1) The medical officer shall regularly inspect and advise the director upon:

a) The quantity, quality, preparation and service of food;

b) The hygiene and cleanliness of the institution and the prisoners;

c) The sanitation, heating, lighting and ventilation of the institution;

d) The suitability and cleanliness of the prisoners' clothing and bedding;

e) The observance of the rules concerning physical education and sports, in cases where there is no technical personnel in charge of these activities.

(2) The director shall take into consideration the reports and advice that the medical officer submits according to rules 25 (2) and 26 and, in case he concurs with the recommendations made, shall take immediate steps to give effect to those recommendations; if they are not within his competence or if he does not concur with them, he shall immediately submit his own report and the advice of the medical officer to higher authority.

Discipline and punishment

27. Discipline and order shall be maintained with firmness, but with no more restriction than is necessary for safe custody and well-ordered community life.

28. (1) No prisoner shall be employed, in the service of the institution, in any disciplinary capacity.

(2) This rule shall not, however, impede the proper functioning of systems based on self-government, under which specified social, educational or sports activities or responsibilities are entrusted, under supervision, to prisoners who are formed into groups for the purposes of treatment.

29. The following shall always be determined by the law or by the regulation of the competent administrative authority:

a) Conduct constituting a disciplinary offence;

b) The types and duration of punishment which may be inflicted;

c) The authority competent to impose such punishment.

30. (1) No prisoner shall be punished except in accordance with the terms of such law or regulation, and never twice for the same offence.

(2) No prisoner shall be punished unless he has been informed of the offence alleged against him and given a proper opportunity of presenting his defence. The competent authority shall conduct a thorough examination of the case.

(3) Where necessary and practicable the prisoner shall be allowed to make his defence through an interpreter.

31. Corporal punishment, punishment by placing in a dark cell, and all cruel, inhuman or degrading punishment shall be completely prohibited as punishments for disciplinary offences.

32. (1) Punishment by close confinement or reduction of diet shall never be inflicted unless the medical officer has examined the prisoner and certified in writing that he is fit to sustain it.

(2) The same shall apply to any other punishment that may be prejudicial to the physical or mental health of a prisoner. In no case may such punishment be contrary to or depart from the principle stated in rule 31.

(3) The medical officer shall visit daily prisoners undergoing such punishments and shall advise the director if he considers the termination or alteration of the punishment necessary on grounds of physical or mental health.

Instruments of restraint

33. Instruments of restraint, such as handcuffs, chains, irons and straitjackets, shall never be applied as a punishment. Furthermore, chains or irons shall not be used as restraints. Other instruments of restraint shall not be used except in the following circumstances:

a) As a precaution against escape during a transfer, provided that they shall be removed when the prisoner appears before a judicial or administrative authority;

b) On medical grounds by direction of the medical officer;

c) By order of the director, if other methods of control fail, in order to prevent a prisoner from injuring himself or others or from damaging property; in such instances the director shall at once consult the medical officer and report to the higher administrative authority.

34. The patterns and manner of use of instruments of restraint shall be decided by the central prison administration. Such instruments must not be applied for any longer time than is strictly necessary.

Information to and complaints by prisoners

35. (1) Every prisoner on admission shall be provided with written information about the regulations governing the treatment of prisoners of his

category, the disciplinary requirements of the institution, the authorized methods of seeking information and making complaints, and all such other matters as are necessary to enable him to understand both his rights and his obligations and to adapt himself to the life of the institution.

(2) If a prisoner is illiterate, the aforesaid information shall be conveyed to him orally.

36. (1) Every prisoner shall have the opportunity each week day of making requests or complaints to the director of the institution or the officer authorized to represent him.

(2) It shall be possible to make requests or complaints to the inspector of prisons during his inspection. The prisoner shall have the opportunity to talk to the inspector or to any other inspecting officer without the director or other members of the staff being present.

(3) Every prisoner shall be allowed to make a request or complaint, without censorship as to substance but in proper form, to the central prison administration, the judicial authority, or other proper authorities through approved channels.

(4) Unless it is evidently frivolous or groundless, every request or complaint shall be promptly dealt with and replied to without undue delay.

Contact with the outside world

37. Prisoners shall be allowed under necessary supervision to communicate with their family and reputable friends at regular intervals, both by correspondence and by receiving visits.

38. (1) Prisoners who are foreign nationals shall be allowed reasonable facilities to communicate with the diplomatic and consular representatives of the State to which they belong.

(2) Prisoners who are nationals of States without diplomatic or consular representation in the country and refugees or stateless persons shall be allowed similar facilities to communicate with the diplomatic representative of the State which takes charge of their interests or any national or international authority whose task it is to protect such persons.

39. Prisoners shall be kept informed regularly of the more important items of news by the reading of newspapers, periodicals or special institutional publications, by hearing wireless transmissions, by lectures or by any similar means as authorized or controlled by the administration.

Books

40. Every institution shall have a library for the use of all categories of prisoners, adequately stocked with both recreational and instructional books, and prisoners shall be encouraged to make full use of it.

Religion

41. (1) If the institution contains a sufficient number of prisoners of the same religion, a qualified representative of that religion shall be appointed or approved. If the number of prisoners justifies it and conditions permit, the arrangement should be on a full-time basis.

(2) A qualified representative appointed or approved under paragraph 1) shall be allowed to hold regular services and to pay pastoral visits in private to prisoners of his religion at proper times.

(3) Access to a qualified representative of any religion shall not be refused to any prisoner. On the other hand, if any prisoner should object to a visit of any religious representative, his attitude shall be fully respected.

42. So far as practicable, every prisoner shall be allowed to satisfy the needs of his religious life by attending the services provided in the institution and having in his possession the books of religious observance and instruction of his denomination.

Retention of prisoners' property

43. (1) All money, valuables, clothing and other effects belonging to a prisoner which under the regulations of the institution he is not allowed to retain shall on his admission to the institution be placed in safe custody. An inventory thereof shall be signed by the prisoner. Steps shall be taken to keep them in good condition,

(2) On the release of the prisoner all such articles and money shall be returned to him except in so far as he has been authorized to spend money or send any such property out of the institution, or it has been found necessary on hygienic grounds to destroy any article of clothing. The prisoner shall sign a receipt for the articles and money returned to him.

(3) Any money or effects received for a prisoner from outside shall be treated in the same way.

(4) If a prisoner brings in any drugs or medicine, the medical officer shall decide what use shall be made of them.

Notification of death, illness, transfer, etc

44. (1) Upon the death or serious illness of, or serious injury to a prisoner, or his removal to an institution for the treatment of mental affections, the director shall at once inform the spouse, if the prisoner is

married, or the nearest relative and shall in any event inform any other person previously designated by the prisoner.

(2) A prisoner shall be informed at once of the death or serious illness of any near relative. In case of the critical illness of a near relative, the prisoner should be authorized, whenever circumstances allow, to go to his bedside either under escort or alone.

(3) Every prisoner shall have the right to inform at once his family of his imprisonment or his transfer to another institution.

Removal of prisoners

45. (1) When prisoners are being removed to or from an institution, they shall be exposed to public view as little as possible, and proper safeguards shall be adopted to protect them from insult, curiosity and publicity in any form.

(2) The transport of prisoners in conveyances with inadequate ventilation or light, or in any way which would subject them to unnecessary physical hardship, shall be prohibited.

(3) The transport of prisoners shall be carried out at the expense of the administration and equal conditions shall obtain for all of them. [...]

Institutional personnel

48. All members of the personnel shall at all times so conduct themselves and perform their duties as to influence the prisoners for good by their example and to command their respect.

49. (1) So far as possible the personnel shall include a sufficient number of specialists such as psychiatrists, psychologists, social workers, teachers and trade instructors.

(2) The services of social workers, teachers and trade instructors shall be secured on a permanent basis, without thereby excluding part-time or voluntary workers. [...]

52. (1) In institutions which are large enough to require the services of one or more full-time medical officers, at least one of them shall reside on the premises of the institution or in its immediate vicinity.

(2) In other institutions the medical officer shall visit daily and shall reside near enough to be able to attend without delay in cases of urgency.

53. (1) In an institution for both men and women, the part of the institution set aside for women shall be under the authority of a responsible woman officer who shall have the custody of the keys of all that part of the institution.

(2) No male member of the staff shall enter the part of the institution set aside for women unless accompanied by a woman officer.

(3) Women prisoners shall be attended and supervised only by women officers. This does not, however, preclude male members of the staff, particularly doctors and teachers, from carrying out their professional duties in institutions or parts of institutions set aside for women.

54. (1) Officers of the institutions shall not, in their relations with the prisoners, use force except in self-defence or in cases of attempted escape, or active or passive physical resistance to an order based on law or regulations. Officers who have recourse to force must use no more than is strictly necessary and must report the incident immediately to the director of the institution.

(2) Prison officers shall be given special physical training to enable them to restrain aggressive prisoners.

(3) Except in special circumstances, staff performing duties which bring them into direct contact with prisoners should not be armed. Furthermore, staff should in no circumstances be provided with arms unless they have been trained in their use.

Inspection

55. There shall be a regular inspection of penal institutions and services by qualified and experienced inspectors appointed by a competent authority. Their task shall be in particular to ensure that these institutions are administered in accordance with existing laws and regulations and with a view to bringing about the objectives of penal and correctional services.

Part II. Rules applicable to special categories

A. Prisoners under sentence

Guiding principles

56. The guiding principles hereafter are intended to show the spirit in which penal institutions should be administered and the purposes at which they should aim, in accordance with the declaration made under Preliminary Observation 1 of the present text.

57. Imprisonment and other measures which result in cutting off an offender from the outside world are afflictive by the very fact of taking from the person the right of self-determination by depriving him of his liberty. Therefore the prison system shall not, except as incidental to justifiable

segregation or the maintenance of discipline, aggravate the suffering inherent in such a situation.

58. The purpose and justification of a sentence of imprisonment or a similar measure deprivative of liberty is ultimately to protect society against crime. This end can only be achieved if the period of imprisonment is used to ensure, so far as possible, that upon his return to society the offender is not only willing but able to lead a law-abiding and self-supporting life.

59. To this end, the institution should utilize all the remedial, educational, moral, spiritual and other forces and forms of assistance which are appropriate and available and should seek to apply them according to the individual treatment needs of the prisoners.

60. (1) The regime of the institution should seek to minimize any differences between prison life and life at liberty which tend to lessen the responsibility of the prisoners or the respect due to their dignity as human beings.

(2) Before the completion of the sentence, it is desirable that the necessary steps be taken to ensure for the prisoner a gradual return to life in society. This aim may be achieved, depending on the case, by a pre-release regime organized in the same institution or in another appropriate institution, or by release on trial under some kind of supervision which must not be entrusted to the police but should be combined with effective social aid.

61. The treatment of prisoners should emphasize not their exclusion from the community but their continuing part in it. Community agencies should, therefore, be enlisted wherever possible to assist the staff of the institution in the task of social rehabilitation of the prisoners. There should be in connexion with every institution social workers charged with the duty of maintaining and improving all desirable relations of a prisoner with his family and with valuable social agencies. Steps should be taken to safeguard to the maximum extent compatible with the law and the sentence, the rights relating to civil interests, social security rights and other social benefits of prisoners.

62. The medical services of the institution shall seek to detect and shall treat any physical or mental illnesses or defects which may hamper a prisoner's rehabilitation. All necessary medical, surgical and psychiatric services shall be provided to that end. [...]

Treatment

65. The treatment of persons sentenced to imprisonment or a similar measure shall have as its purpose, so far as the length of the sentence permits, to establish in them the will to lead law-abiding and self-supporting

lives after their release and to fit them to do so. The treatment shall be such as will encourage their self-respect and develop their sense of responsibility.

66. (1) To these ends all appropriate means shall be used, including religious care in the countries where this is possible, education, vocational guidance and training, social casework, employment counselling, physical development and strengthening of moral character, in accordance with the individual needs of each prisoner, taking account of his social and criminal history, his physical and mental capacities and aptitudes, his personal temperament, the length of his sentence and his prospects after release.

(2) For every prisoner with a sentence of suitable length, the director shall receive, as soon as possible after his admission, full reports on all the matters referred to in the foregoing paragraph. Such reports shall always include a report by a medical officer, wherever possible qualified in psychiatry, on the physical and mental condition of the prisoner.

(3) The reports and other relevant documents shall be placed in an individual file. This file shall be kept up to date and classified in such a way that it can be consulted by the responsible personnel whenever the need arises. [...]

Work

71. (1) Prison labour must not be of an afflictive nature.

(2) All prisoners under sentence shall be required to work, subject to their physical and mental fitness as determined by the medical officer.

(3) Sufficient work of a useful nature shall be provided to keep prisoners actively employed for a normal working day.

(4) So far as possible the work provided shall be such as will maintain or increase the prisoner's ability to earn an honest living after release.

(5) Vocational training in useful trades shall be provided for prisoners able to profit thereby and especially for young prisoners.

(6) Within the limits compatible with proper vocational selection and with the requirements of institutional administration and discipline, the prisoners shall be able to choose the type of work they wish to perform.

72. (1) The organization and methods of work in the institutions shall resemble as closely as possible those of similar work outside institutions, so as to prepare prisoners for the conditions of normal occupational life.

(2) The interests of the prisoners and of their vocational training, however, must not be subordinated to the purpose of making a financial profit from an industry in the institution. [...]

Education and recreation

77. (1) Provision shall be made for the further education of all prisoners capable of profiting thereby, including religious instruction in the countries where this is possible. The education of illiterates and young prisoners shall be compulsory and special attention shall be paid to it by the administration.

(2) So far as practicable, the education of prisoners shall be integrated with the educational system of the country so that after their release they may continue their education without difficulty.

78. Recreational and cultural activities shall be provided in all institutions for the benefit of the mental and physical health of prisoners.

Social relations and after-care

79. Special attention shall be paid to the maintenance and improvement of such relations between a prisoner and his family as are desirable in the best interests of both.

80. From the beginning of a prisoner's sentence consideration shall be given to his future after release and he shall be encouraged and assisted to maintain or establish such relations with persons or agencies outside the institution as may promote the best interests of his family and his own social rehabilitation. [...]

B. Insane and mentally abnormal prisoners

82. (1) Persons who are found to be insane shall not be detained in prisons and arrangements shall be made to remove them to mental institutions as soon as possible.

(2) Prisoners who suffer from other mental diseases or abnormalities shall be observed and treated in specialized institutions under medical management.

(3) During their stay in a prison, such prisoners shall be placed under the special supervision of a medical officer.

(4) The medical or psychiatric service of the penal institutions shall provide for the psychiatric treatment of all other prisoners who are in need of such treatment.

83. It is desirable that steps should be taken, by arrangement with the appropriate agencies, to ensure if necessary the continuation of psychiatric treatment after release and the provision of social-psychiatric after-care.

C. Prisoners under arrest or awaiting trial

84. (1) Persons arrested or imprisoned by reason of a criminal charge against them, who are detained either in police custody or in prison custody (jail) but have not yet been tried and sentenced, will be referred to as "untried prisoners" hereinafter in these rules.

(2) Unconvicted prisoners are presumed to be innocent and shall be treated as such.

(3) Without prejudice to legal rules for the protection of individual liberty or prescribing the procedure to be observed in respect of untried prisoners, these prisoners shall benefit by a special regime which is described in the following rules in its essential requirements only.

85. (1) Untried prisoners shall be kept separate from convicted prisoners.

(2) Young untried prisoners shall be kept separate from adults and shall in principle be detained in separate institutions.

86. Untried prisoners shall sleep singly in separate rooms, with the reservation of different local custom in respect of the climate.

87. Within the limits compatible with the good order of the institution, untried prisoners may, if they so desire, have their food procured at their own expense from the outside, either through the administration or through their family or friends. Otherwise, the administration shall provide their food.

88. (1) An untried prisoner shall be allowed to wear his own clothing if it is clean and suitable.

(2) If he wears prison dress, it shall be different from that supplied to convicted prisoners.

89. An untried prisoner shall always be offered opportunity to work, but shall not be required to work. If he chooses to work, he shall be paid for it.

90. An untried prisoner shall be allowed to procure at his own expense or at the expense of a third party such books, newspapers, writing materials and other means of occupation as are compatible with the interests of the administration of justice and the security and good order of the institution.

91. An untried prisoner shall be allowed to be visited and treated by his own doctor or dentist if there is reasonable ground for his application and he is able to pay any expenses incurred.

92. An untried prisoner shall be allowed to inform immediately his family of his detention and shall be given all reasonable facilities for communicating with his family and friends, and for receiving visits from them, subject only to such restrictions and supervision as are necessary in the interests of the administration of justice and of the security and good order of the institution.

93. For the purposes of his defence, an untried prisoner shall be allowed to apply for free legal aid where such aid is available, and to receive visits from his legal adviser with a view to his defence and to prepare and hand to him confidential instructions. For these purposes, he shall if he so desires be supplied with writing material. Interviews between the prisoner and his legal adviser may be within sight but not within hearing of a police or institution official.

D. Civil prisoners

94. In countries where the law permits imprisonment for debt, or by order of a court under any other non-criminal process, persons so imprisoned shall not be subject to any greater restriction or severity than is necessary to ensure safe custody and good order. Their treatment shall be not less favourable than that of untried prisoners, with the reservation, however, that they may possibly be required to work.

E. Persons arrested or detained without charge

95. Without prejudice to the provisions of article 9 of the International Covenant on Civil and Political Rights, persons arrested or imprisoned without charge shall be accorded the same protection as that accorded under part I and part II, section C. Relevant provisions of part II, section A, shall likewise be applicable where their application may be conducive to the benefit of this special group of persons in custody, provided that no measures shall be taken implying that re-education or rehabilitation is in any way appropriate to persons not convicted of any criminal offence.

Annex

Procedures for the Effective Implementation of the Standard Minimum Rules for the Treatment of Prisoners

Procedure 1

All States whose standards for the protection of all persons subjected to any form of detention or imprisonment fall short of the Standard Minimum Rules for the Treatment of Prisoners shall adopt the Rules.

Procedure 2

Subject, as necessary, to their adaptation to the existing laws and culture but without deviation from the spirit and purpose of the Rules, the Standard Minimum Rules shall be embodied in national legislation and other regulations.

Procedure 3

The Standard Minimum Rules shall be made available to all persons concerned, particularly to law enforcement officials and correctional personnel, for purposes of enabling their application and execution in the criminal justice system.

Procedure 4

The Standard Minimum Rules, as embodied in national legislation and other regulations, shall also be made available and understandable to all prisoners and all persons under detention, on their admission and during their confinement.

Procedure 5

States shall inform the Secretary-General of the United Nations every five years of the extent of the implementation and the progress made with regard to the application of the Standard Minimum Rules, and of the factors and difficulties, if any, affecting their implementation, by responding to the Secretary-General's questionnaire. [...]

Procedure 6

As part of the information mentioned in procedure 5 above, States should provide the Secretary-General with:

a) Copies or abstracts of all laws, regulations and administrative measures concerning the application of the Standard Minimum Rules to persons under detention and to places and programmes of detention;

b) Any data and descriptive material on treatment programmes, personnel and the number of persons under any form of detention, and statistics, if available;

c) Any other relevant information on the implementation of the Rules, as well as information on the possible difficulties in their application.

Procedure 7

The Secretary-General shall disseminate the Standard Minimum Rules and the present implementing procedures in as many languages as possible, and make them available to all States and intergovernmental and non-governmental organizations concerned, in order to ensure the widest circulation of the Rules and the present implementing procedures.

Procedure 8

The Secretary-General shall disseminate his reports on the implementation of the Rules [...]

Procedure 9

The Secretary-General shall ensure the widest possible reference to and use of the text of the Standard Minimum Rules by the United Nations in all its relevant programmes, including technical co-operation activities.

Procedure 10

As part of its technical co-operation and development programmes the United Nations shall:

a) Aid Governments, at their request, in setting up and strengthening comprehensive and humane correctional systems;

b) Make available to Governments requesting them the services of experts and regional and interregional advisers on crime prevention and criminal justice;

c) Promote national and regional seminars and other meetings at the professional and non-professional levels to further the dissemination of the Standard Minimum Rules and the present implementing procedures;

d) Strengthen substantive support to regional research and training institutes in crime prevention and criminal justice that are associated with the United Nations.

The United Nations regional research and training institutes in crime prevention and criminal justice, in co-operation with national institutions, shall develop curricula and training materials, based on the Standard Minimum Rules and the present implementing procedures, suitable for use in criminal justice educational programmes at all levels, as well as in specialized courses on human rights and other related subjects.

Procedure 11

The United Nations Committee on Crime Prevention and Control shall:

a) Keep under review, from time to time, the Standard Minimum Rules, with a view to the elaboration of new rules, standards and procedures applicable to the treatment of persons deprived of liberty;

b) Follow up the present implementing procedures, including periodic reporting under procedure 5 above.

Procedure 12

The Committee on Crime Prevention and Control shall assist the General Assembly, the Economic and Social Council and any other United Nations human rights bodies, as appropriate, with recommendations relating to reports of *ad hoc* inquiry commissions, with respect to matters pertaining to the application and implementation of the Standard Minimum Rules.

Procedure 13

Nothing in the present implementing procedures should be construed as precluding resort to any other means or remedies available under international law or set forth by other United Nations bodies and agencies for the redress of violations of human rights, including the procedure on consistent patterns of gross violations of human rights under Economic and Social Council resolution 1503 (XLVIII) of 27 May 1970, the communication procedure under the Optional Protocol to the International Covenant on Civil and Political Rights and the communication procedure under the International Convention on the Elimination of All Forms of Racial Discrimination.

Amnesty International Declarations and Programs

- Declaration of Stockholm
(Conference on the abolition of the death penalty)

- Declaration on the participation of
health personnel in the death penalty

- 12 point program for the prevention of torture

- 14 point program for the prevention
of extrajudicial executions

- 14 point program for the prevention
of disappearances

Conference on the Abolition of the Death Penalty: Declaration of Stockholm

(Amnesty International, 11 December 1977)

The Stockholm Conference on the Abolition of the Death Penalty, composed of more than 200 delegates and participants from Africa, Asia, Europe, the Middle East, North and South America and the Caribbean region,

Recalls that:
- The death penalty is the ultimate cruel, inhuman and degrading punishment and violates the right to life.

Considers that:
- The death penalty is frequently used as an instrument of repression against opposition, racial, ethnic, religious and underprivileged groups,
- Execution is an act of violence, and violence tends to provoke violence,
- The imposition and infliction of the death penalty is brutalizing to all who are involved in the process,
- The death penalty has never been shown to have a special deterrent effect,
- The death penalty is increasingly taking the form of unexplained disappearances, extra-judicial executions and political murders,
- Execution is irrevocable and can be inflicted on the innocent.

Affirms that:
- It is the duty of the state to protect the life of all persons within its jurisdiction without exception,
- Executions for the purposes of political coercion, whether by government agencies or others, are equally unacceptable,
- Abolition of the death penalty is imperative for the achievement of declared international standards.

Declares:
- Its total and unconditional opposition to the death penalty,
- Its condemnation of all executions, in whatever form, committed or condoned by governments,
- Its commitment to work for the universal abolition of the death penalty.

Calls upon:

- Non-governmental organizations, both national and international, to work collectively and individually to provide public information materials directed towards the abolition of the death penalty,
- All governments to bring about the immediate and total abolition of the death penalty,
- The United Nations unambiguously to declare that the death penalty is contrary to international law.

Declaration on the Participation of
Health Personnel in the Death Penalty
(Amnesty International, 1981, 1988)

Amnesty International,

Recalling
that the spirit of the Hippocratic Oath enjoins doctors to practice for the good
of their patients and never to do harm,

Considering
that the Declaration of Tokyo of the World Medical Association provides that
"the utmost respect for human life is to be maintained even under threat, and
no use made of any medical knowledge contrary to the laws of humanity",

Further considering
that the World Medical Association, meeting in Lisbon in 1981, resolved that
it is unethical for physicians to participate in capital punishment,

Noting
that the United Nations' Principles of Medical Ethics enjoin health personnel,
particularly physicians, to refuse to enter into any relationship with a prisoner
other than one directed at evaluating, protecting or improving their physical
and mental health,

Conscious of
the ethical dilemmas posed for health personnel called on to treat or testify
about the condition of prisoners facing capital charges or sentenced to death,
where actions by such personnel could help save the prisoner's life but could
also result in the prisoner's execution,

Mindful
that health personnel can be called on to participate in executions by, *inter
alia*:
  • determining mental and physical fitness for execution,
  • preparing, administering, supervising or advising others on any
    procedure related to execution,

  • making medical examinations during executions, so that an execution can
continue if the prisoner is not yet dead,

Declares
that the participation of health personnel in executions is a violation of professional ethics;

Calls upon
health personnel not to participate in executions;

Further calls upon
organizations of health professionals:
- to protect health personnel who refuse to participate in executions
- to adopt resolutions to these ends, and
- to promote worldwide adherence to these standards.

--oOo--

This declaration was formulated by the Medical Advisory Board of Amnesty International in 1981 and revised in 1988 in the light of developments on the issue.

113

12-Point Program for the Prevention of Torture
(Amnesty International, 1983)

Amnesty International calls on all governments to implement the following 12-Point Program for the Prevention of Torture. It invites concerned individuals and organizations to join in promoting the program. Amnesty International believes that the implementation of these measures is a positive indication of a government's commitment to abolish torture and to work for its abolition worldwide.

1. Official condemnation of torture.

The highest authorities of every country should demonstrate their total opposition to torture. They should make clear to all law enforcement personnel that torture will not be tolerated under any circumstances.

2. Limits on incommunicado detention.

Torture often takes place while the victims are held incommunicado — unable to contact people outside who could help them or find out what is happening to them. Governments should adopt safeguards to ensure that incommunicado detention does not become an opportunity for torture. It is vital that all prisoners be brought before a judicial authority promptly after being taken into custody and that relatives, lawyers and doctors have prompt and regular access to them.

3. No secret detention.

In some countries torture takes place in secret centres, often after the victims are made to "disappear". Governments should ensure that prisoners are held in publicly recognized places, and that accurate information about their whereabouts is made available to relatives and lawyers.

4. Safeguards during interrogation and custody.

Governments should keep procedures for detention and interrogation under regular review. All prisoners should be promptly told of their rights, including the right to lodge complaints about their treatment. There should be regular independent visits of inspection to places of detention. An important safeguard against torture would be the separation of authorities responsible for detention from those in charge of interrogation.

5. Independent investigation of reports of torture.

Governments should ensure that all complaints and reports of torture are impartially and effectively investigated. The methods and findings of such investigations should be made public. Complainants and witnesses should be protected from intimidation.

6. No use of statements extracted under torture.

Governments should ensure that confessions or other evidence obtained through torture may never be invoked in legal proceedings.

7. Prohibition of torture in law.

Governments should ensure that acts of torture are punishable offenses under the criminal law. In accordance with international law, the prohibition of torture must not be suspended under any circumstances, including states of war or other public emergency.

8. Prosecution of alleged torturers.

Those responsible for torture should be brought to justice. This principle should apply wherever they happen to be, wherever the crime was committed and whatever the nationality of the perpetrators or victims. There should be no "safe haven" for torturers.

9. Training procedures.

It should be made clear during the training of all officials involved in the custody, interrogation or treatment of prisoners that torture is a criminal act. They should be instructed that they are obliged to refuse to obey any order to torture.

10. Compensation and rehabilitation.

Victims of torture and their dependants should be entitled to obtain financial compensation. Victims should be provided with appropriate medical care or rehabilitation.

11. International response.

Governments should use all available channels to intercede with governments accused of torture. Inter-governmental mechanisms should be established and used to investigate reports of torture urgently and to take effective action against it. Governments should ensure that military, security or police transfers or training do not facilitate the practice of torture.

12. Ratification of international instruments.

All governments should ratify international instruments containing safeguards and remedies against torture, including the International Covenant on Civil and Political Rights and its Optional Protocol which provides for individual complaints.

14-Point Program for the Prevention of Extrajudicial Executions

(Amnesty International, 1992)

Extrajudicial executions are fundamental violations of human rights and an affront to the conscience of humanity. These unlawful and deliberate killings, carried out by order of a government or with its complicity or acquiescence, have been condemned by the United Nations. Yet extrajudicial executions continue, daily and across the globe.

Many of the victims have been taken into custody or made to "disappear" before being killed. Some are killed in their homes, or in the course of military operations. Some are assassinated by uniformed members of the security forces, or by "death squads" operating with official connivance. Others are killed in peaceful demonstrations.

The accountability of governments for extrajudicial executions is not diminished by the commission of similar abhorrent acts by armed opposition groups. Urgent action is needed to stop extrajudicial executions and bring those responsible to justice.

Amnesty International calls on all governments to implement the following 14-Point Program for the Prevention of Extrajudicial Executions. It invites concerned individuals and organizations to join in promoting the program. Amnesty International believes that the implementation of these measures is a positive indication of a government's commitment to stop extrajudicial executions and to work for their eradication worldwide.

1. Official condemnation

The highest authorities of every country should demonstrate their total opposition to extrajudicial executions. They should make clear to all members of the police, military and other security forces that extrajudicial executions will not be tolerated under any circumstances.

2. Chain-of-command control

Those in charge of the security forces should maintain strict chain-of-command control to ensure that officers under their command do not commit extrajudicial executions. Officials with chain-of-command responsibility who order or tolerate extrajudicial executions by those under their command should be held criminally responsible for these acts.

3. Restraints on use of force
Governments should ensure that law enforcement officials use force only when strictly necessary and only to the minimum extent required under the circumstances. Lethal force should not be used except when strictly unavoidable in order to protect life.

4. Action against "death squads"
"Death squads", private armies, criminal gangs and paramilitary forces operating outside the chain of command but with official support or acquiescence should be prohibited and disbanded. Members of such groups who have perpetrated extrajudicial executions should be brought to justice.

5. Protection against death threats
Governments should ensure that anyone in danger of extrajudicial execution, including those who receive death threats, is effectively protected.

6. No secret detention
Governments should ensure that prisoners are held only in publicly recognized places of detention and that accurate information about the arrest and detention of any prisoner is made available promptly to relatives, lawyers and the courts. No one should be secretly detained.

7. Access to prisoners
All prisoners should be brought before a judicial authority without delay after being taken into custody. Relatives, lawyers and doctors should have prompt and regular access to them. There should be regular, independent, unannounced and unrestricted visits of inspection to all places of detention.

8. Prohibition in law
Governments should ensure that the commission of an extrajudicial execution is a criminal offence, punishable by sanctions commensurate with the gravity of the practice. The prohibition of extrajudicial executions and the essential safeguards for their prevention must not be suspended under any circumstances, including states of war or other public emergency.

9. Individual responsibility
The prohibition of extrajudicial executions should be reflected in the training of all officials involved in the arrest and custody of prisoners and all officials authorized to use lethal force, and in the instructions issued to them. These officials should be instructed that they have the right and duty to refuse to obey any order to participate in an extrajudicial execution. An order from a superior officer or a public authority must never be invoked as a justification for taking part in an extrajudicial execution.

10. Investigation

Governments should ensure that all complaints and reports of extrajudicial executions are investigated promptly, impartially and effectively by a body which is independent of those allegedly responsible and has the necessary powers and resources to carry out the investigation. The methods and findings of the investigation should be made public. The body of the alleged victim should not be disposed of until an adequate autopsy has been conducted by a suitably qualified doctor who is able to function impartially. Officials suspected of responsibility for extrajudicial executions should be suspended from active duty during the investigation. Relatives of the victim should have access to information relevant to the investigation, should be entitled to appoint their own doctor to carry out or be present at an autopsy, and should be entitled to present evidence. Complainants, witnesses, lawyers, judges and others involved in the investigation should be protected from intimidation and reprisals.

11. Prosecution

Governments should ensure that those responsible for extrajudicial executions are brought to justice. This principle should apply wherever such people happen to be, wherever the crime was committed, whatever the nationality of the perpetrators or victims and no matter how much time has elapsed since the commission of the crime. Trials should be in the civilian courts. The perpetrators should not be allowed to benefit from any legal measures exempting them from criminal prosecution or conviction.

12. Compensation

Dependants of victims of extrajudicial execution should be entitled to obtain fair and adequate redress from the state, including financial compensation.

13. Ratification of human rights treaties and implementation of international standards

All governments should ratify international treaties containing safeguards and remedies against extrajudicial executions, including the International Covenant on Civil and Political Rights and its first Optional Protocol which provides for individual complaints. Governments should ensure full implementation of the relevant provisions of these and other international instruments, including the UN Principles on the Effective Prevention and Investigation of Extra-Legal, Arbitrary and Summary Executions, and comply with the recommendations of intergovernmental organizations concerning these abuses.

14. **International responsibility**

Governments should use all available channels to intercede with the governments of countries where extrajudicial executions have been reported. They should ensure that training and transfers of equipment, know-how and training for military, security or police use do not facilitate extrajudicial executions. No one should be forcibly returned to a country where he or she risks becoming a victim of extrajudicial execution.

14-Point Program for the Prevention of "Disappearances"

(Amnesty International, 1992)

The "disappeared" are people who have been taken into custody by agents of the state, yet whose whereabouts and fate are concealed, and whose custody is denied. "Disappearances" cause agony for the victims and their relatives. The victims are cut off from the world and placed outside the protection of the law; often they are tortured; many are never seen again. Their relatives are kept in ignorance, unable to find out whether the victims are alive or dead.

The United Nations has condemned "disappearances" as a grave violation of human rights and has said that their systematic practice is of the nature of a crime against humanity. Yet thousands of people "disappear" each year across the globe, and countless others remain "disappeared". Urgent action is needed to stop "disappearances", to clarify the fate of the "disappeared" and to bring those responsible to justice.

Amnesty International calls on all governments to implement the following 14-Point Program for the Prevention of "Disappearances". It invites concerned individuals and organizations to join in promoting the program. Amnesty International believes that the implementation of these measures is a positive indication of a government's commitment to stop "disappearances" and to work for their eradication worldwide.

1. Official condemnation

The highest authorities of every country should demonstrate their total opposition to "disappearances". They should make clear to all members of the police, military and other security forces that "disappearances" will not be tolerated under any circumstances.

2. Chain-of-command control

Those in charge of the security forces should maintain strict chain-of-command control to ensure that officers under their command do not commit "disappearances". Officials with chain-of-command responsibility who order or tolerate "disappearances" by those under their command should be held criminally responsible for these acts.

3. Information on detention and release
Accurate information about the arrest of any person and about his or her place of detention, including transfers and releases, should be made available promptly to relatives, lawyers and the courts. Prisoners should be released in a way that allows reliable verification of their release and ensures their safety.

4. Mechanism for locating and protecting prisoners
Governments should at all times ensure that effective judicial remedies are available which enable relatives and lawyers to find out immediately where a prisoner is held and under what authority, to ensure his or her safety, and to obtain the release of anyone arbitrarily detained.

5. No secret detention
Governments should ensure that prisoners are held only in publicly recognized places of detention. Up-to-date registers of all prisoners should be maintained in every place of detention and centrally. The information in these registers should be made available to relatives, lawyers, judges, official bodies trying to trace people who have been detained, and others with a legitimate interest. No one should be secretly detained.

6. Authorization of arrest and detention
Arrest and detention should be carried out only by officials who are authorized by law to do so. Officials carrying out an arrest should identify themselves to the person arrested and, on demand, to others witnessing the event. Governments should establish rules setting forth which officials are authorized to order an arrest or detention. Any deviation from established procedures which contributes to a "disappearance" should be punished by appropriate sanctions.

7. Access to prisoners
All prisoners should be brought before a judicial authority without delay after being taken into custody. Relatives, lawyers and doctors should have prompt and regular access to them. There should be regular, independent, unannounced and unrestricted visits of inspection to all places of detention.

8. Prohibition in law
Governments should ensure that the commission of a "disappearance" is a criminal offence, punishable by sanctions commensurate with the gravity of the practice. The prohibition of "disappearances" and the essential safeguards for their prevention must not be suspended under any circumstances, including states of war or other public emergency.

9. Individual responsibility

The prohibition of "disappearances" should be reflected in the training of all officials involved in the arrest and custody of prisoners and in the instructions issued to them. They should be instructed that they have the right and duty to refuse to obey any order to participate in a "disappearance". An order from a superior officer or a public authority must never be invoked as a justification for taking part in a "disappearance".

10. Investigation

Governments should ensure that all complaints and reports of "disappearances" are investigated promptly, impartially and effectively by a body which is independent of those allegedly responsible and has the necessary powers and resources to carry out the investigation. The methods and findings of the investigation should be made public. Officials suspected of responsibility for "disappearances" should be suspended from active duty during the investigation. Relatives of the victim should have access to information relevant to the investigation and should be entitled to present evidence. Complainants, witnesses, lawyers and others involved in the investigation should be protected from intimidation and reprisals. The investigation should not be curtailed until the fate of the victim is officially clarified.

11. Prosecution

Governments should ensure that those responsible for "disappearances" are brought to justice. This principle should apply wherever such people happen to be, wherever the crime was committed, whatever the nationality of the perpetrators or victims and no matter how much time has elapsed since the commission of the crime. Trials should be in the civilian courts. The perpetrators should not benefit from any legal measures exempting them from criminal prosecution or conviction.

12. Compensation and rehabilitation

Victims of "disappearance" and their dependants should be entitled to obtain fair and adequate redress from the state, including financial compensation. Victims who reappear should be provided with appropriate medical care or rehabilitation.

13. Ratification of human rights treaties and implementation of international standards

All governments should ratify international treaties containing safeguards and remedies against "disappearances", including the International Covenant on Civil and Political Rights and its first Optional Protocol which provides for individual complaints. Governments should ensure full implementation of the relevant provisions of these and other international instruments, including the UN Declaration on the Protection of All Persons from Enforced Disappearance, and comply with the recommendations of intergovernmental organizations concerning these abuses.

14. International responsibility

Governments should use all available channels to intercede with the governments of countries where "disappearances" have been reported. They should ensure that transfers of equipment, know-how and training for military, security or police use do not facilitate "disappearances". No one should be forcibly returned to a country where he or she risks being made to "disappear".

Ethical Codes and Declarations Relevant to the Health Professions

An Amnesty International compilation of selected ethical texts

Third revised English edition published in May 1994
by Amnesty International Publications
1 Easton Street, London WC1X 8DJ, United Kingdom

AI Index: ACT 75/04/94
ISBN: 0 86210 233 2